Advance Praise

"A must-read for anyone in sales or supporting sales in senior living. Kelly's discussion of being authentic and the importance of listening are powerful lessons for anyone trying to drive occupancy in their communities. Kelly's wealth of experience is on full display, and the takeaways in her book are truly impactful!"

—TEDDY HELFRICH, VICE PRESIDENT OF
SALES, WELCOMEHOME SOFTWARE

"This book beautifully highlights the importance of curiosity, empathy, and authenticity in senior living sales. Kelly Singleton Myers offers practical and insightful advice that will resonate with any sales professional looking to make a real difference in the lives of seniors."

—RACHEL KELLER, VP OF SALES, SERVIUM CARE NETWORK

"In an age dominated by artificial intelligence, Kelly Singleton Myers demonstrates nothing can replace the value of experience and the wisdom it imparts. *The More You Know, The More You Close: The Power of Curiosity-Driven Sales* provides practical guidance honed over Kelly's extensive career in seniors housing; underscoring the importance of customer-focused behaviors such as empathy and curiosity. Rich with proven strategies, insightful observations, and vivid examples, this book is indispensable for sales professionals aiming to advance their careers and enhance their selling skills."

—JAMISON J. GOSSELIN, EXECUTIVE CONSULTANT, JAMISON MARKETING & COMMUNICATIONS

"They say empathy can't be taught, but Kelly Singleton Myers has found a way to reveal it, strengthen it, and help sales and marketing professionals find it every day, in every interaction. This wonderful book is a must-have not just for senior living sales teams but for anyone responsible for creating a meaningful journey for prospects and their families."

—NATE O'KEEFE, FOUNDER AND CEO, ROOBRIK

The More You Know, The More You Close

The More You Know, The More You Close

The Power of Curiosity-Driven Sales

Kelly Singleton Myers

LIONCREST
PUBLISHING

THE MORE YOU KNOW, THE MORE YOU CLOSE
The Power of Curiosity-Driven Sales

FIRST EDITION

ISBN   978-1-5445-4638-4   *Hardcover*
      978-1-5445-4637-7   *Paperback*
      978-1-5445-4639-1   *Ebook*

To those embarking on the emotional journey of finding the right senior living community—both the individuals seeking a new home and the families supporting them—this book is dedicated to you.

It's my hope that sales professionals who adopt the concepts within these pages will provide you with an experience that's built on empathy, understanding, and genuine care. They are here not just to offer you a place but to guide you toward a community that honors your unique needs and helps you feel truly seen, heard, and valued.

Contents

Contents

Foreword

—David A. Smith, Esq., Principal, The Gatesworth Communities
Founder Sherpa CRM & One on One Services
Author, *It's About Time*
Producer, *Time to Get Ready*

I love senior living and what it does to extend and enhance the lives of its residents! Given the many proven benefits of moving to a senior community, qualified prospects should "sell themselves." Yet, anyone who has ever tried knows that senior living is very difficult to sell. It is a complex, multi-call sale with a strong overlay of emotional resistance. Only about 10 percent of the people who would clearly benefit from living in a community ever actually move.

As a result, communities struggle to fill, and it is not uncommon for sales professionals to become exhausted. Staff turnover is high. Looking to enhance occupancies, most operators rely heavily on social media and lead aggregators to drive as many new inquiries as they can. This approach has the unintended consequence of putting even more pressure on sales professionals to "close" as quickly as possible.

In this book, Kelly Singleton Myers offers a different, more practical, and more rewarding approach to faster fills and to higher occupancies. *The More You Know, the More You Close* fosters authentic connections, builds trust, and inspires higher-functioning prospects to "get ready." Kelly invites us to embrace curiosity as a cornerstone. Curiosity can help us "slow down" in order to help prospects more quickly overcome emotional resistance. Her proven track record drives higher conversion rates with qualified prospects that are already in our lead base. Authentic, empathic selling is also a powerful antidote to sales counselor burnout. The senior living industry really needs this book, now more than ever.

Kelly draws from her impressive experience in healthcare management, hiring and onboarding, sales operations, training, coaching, and home care. For over twenty-three years, Kelly was a sales leader at Sunrise Senior Living, one of the industry's most respected providers. As the founder and chief vision officer of KJB Sales, Kelly knows what it takes to convert prospects, close sales, and, perhaps just as important, what it takes to motivate, coach, and inspire sales professionals.

It should not be surprising that Kelly's curiosity-driven approach comes naturally and draws from her own Midwestern values. Compassion—her passion to nurture and support starts with but also goes way beyond helping other humans. Her love of pets is part of who she is. In my next life, I want to come back as one of Kelly's dogs! Determination—an avid triathlete, Kelly pushes herself to train, compete, and endure with dedication and practice. Commitment to learning—long after she had demonstrated success leading others in senior living sales, Kelly became a student herself when she invited me to come teach and present my own version of Prospect-Centered Selling® to her sales teams. She listened, questioned, supported, and learned.

As a senior living industry leader, regardless of your role, you have an important, difficult job. One that requires the curiosity to gain a deep personal understanding of individual prospects and the compassion and determination to use that understanding to help them navigate a difficult life transition. This book will help you do just that!

Introduction

"Most people do not listen with the intent to understand; they listen with the intent to reply."

—STEPHEN R. COVEY

It's a typical Friday afternoon for Leslie, a Yearly Award Winner for occupancy and rate growth in her senior living community. All day long, she has been on the phone scheduling appointments with customers who will be coming to tour the community. She also has set aside time to schedule business development meetings. And now, her regional director just called and told her she must do a competitor analysis by next week, and her report needs to analyze at least ten competitors.

Twice this week, she had to join focus calls to discuss the challenges her community faces with regards to growing the occupancy. She made fifty calls to prospective residents, and only two people answered the phone. This was discouraging, but she tried to be as creative as possible in all the voicemails she left for the people who didn't answer.

This week has been no different from most weeks—it's no wonder she's exhausted.

Leslie realizes people are depending on her—seniors and their families who have reached the critical, extremely difficult point of knowing they need to find senior living for someone they love. But in the past few weeks, the work has been especially challenging. Even though she has been following her sales plan, referrals have been down over the past month, and Leslie knows she needs to improve the outcomes of her interactions with prospective residents.

She's always understood the pressures of her role. After all, this is sales, and there is always pressure to do more! But lately she's been on more and more calls discussing problems with occupancy, and each time she shares her strategy to grow the occupancy, it feels like it falls on deaf ears. She is frustrated, as the time it takes to join calls and discuss what she's doing is time taken away from doing the work.

Adding to her frustration, it was challenging this past week to get timely assessments completed for two prospective residents who are also looking at several competitor communities.

I'm doing the best I can, she thinks to herself. But the emotional exhaustion took a toll on her this week. Between nurturing relationships with prospective residents, preparing for tailored tours, business development appointments, and the competitor analysis work, she feels as if her cup has runneth over. She is worried she's not giving her best to every customer. She knows they deserve to have her full attention as they embark on making such a difficult decision.

She checks the time and sees it's four o'clock. Only one more hour and then she can go home, watch her favorite show, and unwind. At that moment, she hears the subtle chime of the entrance door as it opens. The community's receptionist asks, "Do you have an appointment?" and a middle-aged woman's voice nervously answers, "No, I just decided to come in and see if I could look around."

Leslie takes a deep breath. She sets aside her feelings of exhaustion and frustration and remembers the critical importance of the role she is about to play for another family. She digs deep and once again finds that caring, competent demeanor, even though what she really wants is for this week to just be over. Leslie understands that everything she does or does not do right now will impact the prospective resident and their family's final decision.

Imagine transforming that exhaustion into excitement by shifting your mindset toward curiosity.

FINDING YOUR PRIORITIES

If Leslie's experience resonates with you, or if as a regional or VP team member you witness these daily struggles, you are not alone. The competing priorities of senior living sales are real. The struggle is real. Your exhaustion is real. It's hard work to balance talking to customers all day in hopes of making a sale while balancing business development duties, administrative duties, and keeping everyone informed of your pipeline for the week and month ahead.

You're working in a world where you need to make sure the person sitting in front of you, the customer, as well as their family, knows that they are your only priority. Their feelings about the experience will impact their decision on whether or not to select your community. But the truth is they're just one of many, many balls you're keeping in the air. Nevertheless, like Leslie, you understand the enormous responsibility you have to each family as they are making one of the most difficult decisions of their lives for someone they love.

There is tremendous pressure on you to grow the occupancy without sacrificing rate for your community. Even more importantly, families are depending on you to solve one of the biggest problems they've ever faced. If you are a community-based seller, you are tasked with a heavy load, especially if you're the only salesperson in the community.

On top of this, the administrative component of this job falls on you, the salesperson. You likely must collect the medical paperwork to gather enough information so that the assessment can be done. You will have to take the lead on discovering any potential issues a prospective resident might have. Can they walk on their own, or do they need a walker or a wheelchair? Are they demonstrating any memory loss? Are they on any kind of special diet? What kinds of food do they like? What are their personal preferences with regard to room location? What hobbies do they enjoy or used to enjoy doing? What are they most looking for in a senior living community? All of these questions have to be answered in order to ensure the community team can provide the services required by the customer.

You may also have all kinds of leads coming in, in which case you will have to pick and choose how to spend your time and energy. How do you decide where to put your focus today, tomorrow, and the next day, all the while keeping speed to lead top of mind? In addition, all those current families who are already considering your community deserve your attention too.

You know you have scheduled actions in your CRM, promises you made to prospective residents and their families. I believe the number one sales rule is "No broken promises."

The name of the game is to build trust.

There are also barriers to sales that are completely out of your control. The senior living market itself fluctuates. There also might be some issues around the intrinsic value of your community. Maybe the amenities are not as fancy as others nearby, or the location isn't that desirable. Any of these things alone will make it tougher to close sales, no matter what you do.

The good news is, it doesn't have to be this difficult or exhausting. It will take a mindset makeover, and this may seem counterintuitive, but you just may have to start caring even more than you already do. By caring, I mean asking the right questions and listening carefully to the answers. I mean being genuinely, authentically interested and motivated to make a connection.

I am asking you to become extremely curious and take a deep, genuine interest in the people you're trying to help. If you keep your sense of curiosity front and center, you'll never be bored. Because just as no two snowflakes are alike, no two human beings are the same, and because of this, you can enjoy an ever-changing experience of really getting to know people.

While these challenges are very real, there is a way to approach them with energy and clarity. A mindset centered around curiosity can help you prioritize what matters most. Just as importantly, this heightened curiosity will boost your sales.

THE POWER OF CURIOSITY

Curiosity and building genuine connections are tough to track and don't always get as much attention as sales metrics, such as new leads to move-ins, tour to move-ins, and new leads to tours. However, in my experience, curiosity-driven sales can significantly increase closing ratios. Many other studies, including several found in the *Harvard Business Review*, also show that fostering curiosity improves outcomes.

This is an area where you can stand out from the competition. We know that most competitors will offer the same basic things—a well-appointed room, vibrant programming, delicious meals, and excellent care. The best way to differentiate your community from the sea of sameness is by focusing on the way prospective residents and their families feel when they interact with you on the phone and visit your community. If you can build genuine connections and show genuine interest based on deep discovery and curiosity, customers will remember how you made them feel. You will stand out.

The key to this is being truly interested; if you're just pretending, it won't work. But if you're really interested in your customers, you'll find that being your authentic self is freeing, and that makes the work easier and more enjoyable. It's simply just not as exhausting to be interested as it is to pretend to be interested. Pretending is extremely exhausting, but truly caring can be extremely fulfilling!

The truth is, prospective residents and their families want to feel seen and heard. This builds a sense of mattering, which we'll discuss later in the book. Building relationships built on trust—being seen and heard—can be a direct ladder to closing more sales.

Additionally, becoming more curious and interested will help you stay more focused. Like reading a good book, you'll have razor sharp focus because you truly want to get to the next page of this person's story. Being focused doesn't make you exhausted; quite the opposite, it gives you energy.

You can't fake being present. If you're truly in the moment with someone, they can tell. If not, they'll know that too. And studies have shown that most sales in this industry are closed based on how the customer (in this case, the prospective resident and their family) feels, not on what they think. So make sure they know you care.

THE VALUE OF AUTHENTICITY

Recently, I was coaching a group of salespeople, and we were discussing how much information they should try to acquire in the inquiry call. One of the participants shared that in her company, the first thing they do is ask the prospective resident or their family about their finances. The reasoning was that if the family couldn't afford their community, they didn't want to waste their time. We then chatted about other ways to gain this information in a timely manner but not necessarily right up front. I've seen families pull resources together when they see what a community can offer and they know this is what their family member deserves.

It may be hard to build rapport if straight out of the gate if you are asking about finances, disregarding their interests and needs. If you listen to learn, you'll have a better chance of creating a compelling reason for them to take the next step. Once I have an opportunity to show the customer what life will be like in our community, I've seen families "find the money." They don't want their loved one to have less than what you can offer.

Another way to demonstrate that you genuinely care is to be nimble enough to meet prospective residents where they are in their journey. Perhaps a prospective resident needs to move in somewhere immediately. You'll need to skip a lot of questions that lead to deep discovery right up front. Your only two questions really need to be "What are you most worried about?" and "What do you need most?"

In any given situation, the important thing is to take the time to get to know the prospective residents as people. You do this by bringing your deepest curiosity from the start. By diligently attempting to understand who this person is and where they are in their journey, you'll make a connection—even before they come to visit the community.

You will find that you can be fascinated with your customers. You can be genuinely interested in people's lives if you just pay attention. These seniors have lived full, interesting, and often fascinating lives. In this book, I'll give you some examples of the fabulous stories I've heard and characters I've met in this work. Their families love them very much and have problems of their own that need to be addressed, and their stories, too, are important.

The key is to create a more compelling reason for your customers to choose your community by creating a feeling. You should strive to create feelings of comfort and ease, warmth, and kindness. And all you have to do is be authentic. Be yourself. Relax and connect. If you do this, combined with the various other aspects of this approach I discuss in this book, you'll see results.

After reading this book, you will understand very clearly how, by being genuine, you will connect more quickly with prospective residents and their families, which will lead to closing more sales. It's as simple as that. Deep discovery—which sometimes involves asking challenging, very personal questions (and this takes courage on your part)—will help you to better personalize the customer's journey through the decision-making process. How energizing it will be when the guardrails are removed and you can take the time to really get to know them, because you are really engaged with their story!

MY STORY

I've spent over three decades in healthcare and senior living, building a career on understanding both the personal and professional challenges people face when making critical decisions about elder care. My journey started in 1989 as a hospital discharge planner. I was responsible for helping patients transition from acute care to other care environments. This role taught me to navigate complex systems, balancing clinical needs with emotional ones—a skill that has shaped my entire career.

After working in admissions and social work within skilled nursing, I found myself on the receiving end of those transitions. I learned first-hand the importance of deep understanding, not just of people's medical conditions but of their emotional needs, their families' fears, and the operational demands of senior living communities. These early roles laid the groundwork for the sales and leadership path I would follow.

In 1999, I moved into the world of senior living as the director of community relations at Sunrise Senior Living. This was a pivotal moment for me—my first foray into the high-stakes, deeply personal world of selling senior living. Over the years, I moved through the ranks, mastering both inside and outside sales. I learned that sales in senior living wasn't just about occupancy rates; it was about building trust, addressing emotions, and offering solutions to families facing some of the hardest decisions they'd ever make.

As my career progressed, I took on more responsibility, overseeing sales in multiple states as a regional sales manager, then growing to vice president of sales. But it was my final role at Sunrise Senior Living, where I spent thirteen years as senior vice president of sales, that truly solidified my expertise. I led sales teams across the US, Canada, and the UK, driving occupancy growth in competitive markets and guiding the teams through the intricacies of selling in a high-emotion, high-risk industry. My tenure saw the creation of innovative programs, including establishing an internal call center and launching a highly effective sales coaching program.

One of the most important lessons I've learned is that selling in senior living is different from any other kind of sales. It's not transactional; it's transformational. The decision to move a loved one into a senior living community is deeply emotional, and the salesperson's role is to act as a trusted guide through that process. This realization became the bedrock of my approach to sales and coaching.

In 2023, after decades of leadership, I co-founded KJB Sales Consulting. My mission? To bring everything I'd learned—every success and every failure—into a consulting firm that would help senior living companies build authentic, Curiosity-Driven Sales cultures. KJB Sales Consulting was born from the belief that great senior living sales leaders don't just drive revenue; they build environments where sales professionals can thrive by putting empathy, trust, and understanding first.

As I reflect on my career, I'm proud of the impact I've had on the industry. I've supported hundreds of communities, coached countless salespeople, and helped families navigate one of life's toughest decisions. And now, with the founding of KJB Sales Consulting, I'm excited to help transform the next generation of senior living sales professionals.

WHY WE DO THIS

To professionalize senior living sales, I want to simplify the success method for you. I want to help you understand that it all just boils down to good manners, great listening skills, patience to learn all you can, and a thorough understanding of the services your community offers. Treat people like they are your friends and family, and they will feel the comfort and ease necessary to choose your community. Your customers have lived a long time, or they have a senior family member who has lived a long time, and these seniors have reached a point where they deserve our respect and true caring. They deserve to have a knowledgeable person helping them through this process, and they deserve our attention. After all, they're looking for a solution to a problem even if they don't fully understand.

In this industry, salespeople often receive more training than other disciplines, but it still hasn't been enough. Perhaps you've gone through a lot of training, but with a lack of consistent coaching on an ongoing basis, the skills can wane. Instead of practicing with colleagues and coaches, you're practicing on the customer, and that's not right, fair, or helpful. Not only do you need to take your sales training seriously but also accept that sales coaching is the tool that will ensure you understand how to use the sales techniques you have learned.

That is one reason why, in this book, I've included practice exercises at the end of each chapter, to help you build the necessary skills and habits to do this work with deep curiosity, authentic interest, and genuine connection. This heightened inquisitiveness will allow you to know more about your customer and thus close more sales.

This book isn't a sales process book. If you are reading this book, I suspect you are already following a sales process, and if we are honest, most "sales processes" have the same core components: build rapport, learn as much as you can about the problem, and tie your services, features, advantages, and benefits to demonstrate how you can best meet their needs. What you'll learn in this book are ways to improve your results with techniques that will take your process to the next level. That means taking a genuine interest and allowing your sales process to be curiosity-driven.

You must be nimble enough to join the customer where they are in their journey, and that takes flexibility and compassion. Sometimes it even means caring more about them than about your commission. It is about slowing down, because ironically, this will propel you toward more sales more quickly. Heeding the lessons outlined in this book will undoubtedly help you close more sales, and, at the same time, it will also enable you to find more meaning and joy in your work as you experience the benefits of working to help others during an extremely difficult time in their lives.

A word about metrics. This book leans heavily into "soft" sales skills such as curiosity, compassion, and empathy. But this is not a self-help book. It is a sales performance book and will most definitely work to positively impact your performance as a salesperson. No matter where in the sales funnel your customers may be, this book is going to help you close more sales and do it more quickly.

Increased sales is the goal, of course, but my method requires that you move that goal to the back burner as you focus more on being truly curious and doggedly learning as much as you can about the people you are helping. Ironically, this is what will get you to the goal the fastest way. Think of enhanced sales performance as the end result and curiosity as the means to get there.

My sincere hope is that learning the approach outlined in this book will remind you of why you got into this business in the first place. Because when you give yourself permission to take the time to really care, you will better understand the enormous responsibility you have in guiding seniors and their families through one of the most difficult times of their lives. I know that much of this may seem contrary to what we are generally taught as salespeople, but in these pages, I will show you the steps and give you the resources so that you can not only grow your occupancy, but you can also enjoy a more meaningful and fulfilling career. You will be truly helping people, and the only way to help someone is to know what their needs are. As we will explore in the next chapter, a family's needs when they are shopping for senior living are made ten times more dire by the fact that they are facing a situation that is so incredibly high-risk and so intensely emotional.

Chapter 1

High Risk, High Emotion

"Vulnerability is not weakness; it's our greatest measure of courage."

—BRENÉ BROWN

Angela, a busy project manager for a mid-size tech firm, has a problem. Her mother, Edith, is eighty-four years old and has stopped taking the shuttle to her local senior center for her weekly knitting club gathering. Edith loves knitting baby beanies for new mothers, and Angela can't figure out why she isn't going anymore. She's also starting to worry her mother will become a shut-in.

Edith has also stopped taking some of her medications, claiming they upset her stomach. Angela lives close by and checks on her mom often, bringing her groceries and taking her to doctors' appointments so often that her supervisor expressed disapproval on her most recent performance review. Her mom's Wednesday afternoon trips to the senior center were one of the few times Angela could catch up on work, but now they've stopped.

Her two sisters and her brother all live in other states and have put her in charge of their mother's care. When it occurred to Angela that her family might need to consider senior living, her siblings disagreed. Angela was torn—she felt immense guilt about even considering senior living but knew deep down it might be the best solution. Her brother insisted their mom was just fine when they were all together last Christmas, and her sisters both talk to their mom once a week and think she's doing just fine on her own. But Angela sees Edith on an almost daily basis, and she knows better. While it's the last thing she's ever wanted to do, she has a sinking feeling she needs to start exploring communities.

When she contacts a few communities to ask some questions, many of the salespeople ask Angela curt questions such as how "ambulatory" her mother is or whether she is "lucid." They make her feel like she's looking for a psychiatric hospital instead of just a decent place for her mom to comfortably live. When Angela mentions her mother's recent issues, one of the salespeople dismisses her concerns as "very common," which doesn't help Angela at all. Overwhelmed with guilt, sadness, and fear over the idea of making such a big change, she's on the verge of giving up and just continuing with things as they are. She decides to try one more place but resolves that if the next place makes her as uncomfortable as all the others, she's going to pause, if not stop, her search.

When she reaches out to another community, the woman on the phone has a kind voice and listens patiently to Angela's story. She seems genuinely interested in helping her instead of just trying to get Angela to tour the place and put down a deposit. The salesperson wants to know if her mom has been eating okay lately. This is where curiosity, not just salesmanship, becomes critical in building trust.

Angela tells her that her mom hasn't been eating well at all lately. In fact, she didn't touch the mashed potatoes this week, even though they are her favorite, and Angela's not sure why. For Angela, and so many other families in her shoes, the risks feel overwhelming. What if they run out of money? What if their Mom is miserable because she can't enjoy the things that used to make her happy? And what about her safety—what if she falls in the middle of the night while trying to make it to the bathroom? These are not just practical concerns; they're emotionally charged, bringing up conflict within the family dynamic. The salesperson then asks something surprising.

"Is it possible your mom may be self-conscious about anything that may keep her from wanting to go to the senior center?" Angela takes a deep breath and shares that her mom has been upset lately about her hygiene, especially making it to the bathroom. She also shares that her mom was always meticulously dressed and always left the house with her hair done and a full face of make-up, and she seems to have lost interest in that as well. She might be feeling sad and lonely over that and even losing her appetite because of it.

Angela hadn't thought to ask herself why her mom might not want to go to the senior center anymore. She realizes she has been thinking more about her own lackluster performance at work than her mother's well-being. But it occurs to her now that her mom might be feeling embarrassed because she's having trouble with incontinence. Angela's emotions—resentments toward other family members because of the situation she's been put in—and her sibling's emotions—concerns over finances and the big decisions they all have to make—now become compounded by their mom's feelings around aging. All this weighs heavily on Angela's shoulders.

She decides she needs to find out the answers to this salesperson's questions. After all, her mom's health and happiness are on the line. She also decides to schedule a tour with this last place, because she feels that out of all the senior living communities she called, this one was different. The person on the phone really cared about helping her mother. Angela will have to "sell" senior living to her siblings, so she's relying on a senior living salesperson to provide all of the information she'll need to persuade them.

THE FAMILY'S STRUGGLES ARE REAL

Because of the highly charged nature of our interactions with families, as senior living salespeople, we have an enormous responsibility to help our customers make decisions. We need to build trust with that family member and realize that the family member also has to build trust with the rest of their family—siblings, usually—so we need to arm that family member with as much truly useful information and as many reasons for their Mom to move to your community. After all, they'll soon be taking that information back to the other family members and presenting it to them.

The risks families are taking at this stage of life are immense. There are financial risks: what if we run out of money? There are emotional risks: what if their Mom is miserable because she can't do any of the things that make her happy? And there are also physical risks: what if she falls in the middle of the night trying to go to the bathroom? All of these highly charged situations can bring a lot of painful conflict within the family dynamic.

Often, as in Angela's case, there is one "token" sibling who shoulders the weight of the decision-making and logistics. While you are trying to sell to her, she will be the one "selling" to everyone else in the family. Angela will be the boots on the ground and do all the groundwork to find the best place. She'll take the tour, and then she'll become the salesperson to the rest of the family. She has four brothers and sisters she needs to convince, and she'll have to work hard to convince them of anything. Their mom is also not excited to leave the home she's lived in for decades and move into a community filled with strangers, so that won't be much fun either.

As a salesperson, you usually only have to sell to that one token sibling, that one adult child. However, that one token sibling has to sell it to the rest of her family, and you need to keep that in mind in all of your interactions. Your responsibility (and opportunity) becomes giving Angela a crystal clear idea of what life will be like for her mom in your community. You need to let her know you won't leave her stranded. Instead, you're going to make sure she has all the information she needs so she can go back to her siblings and their mom and help everyone make this extremely important decision.

So how do you do that?

First, we need to recognize that each time we engage with a new customer, we are walking into a hot mess of emotions. These families are struggling with grief and fear and guilt, and legitimately so. At the same time, we are trying to sell something that has an extremely high price tag. This, of course, only increases all those emotions.

The situation is also complicated by the family dynamics. Not all family members are going to agree about what to do with their Mom or Dad. Different siblings usually have different circumstances as well—they live in different places and have all kinds of different job situations, not to mention personality differences. Sadly, at this point, some adult children also start to think about how this situation is going to impact their inheritance. If there is no inheritance to speak of, they might wonder how much of a drain on their existing finances senior living will be.

I personally have four siblings, and our father recently spent time convalescing in my home for a couple of months. I've been in one area or another of senior living sales for over three decades now, yet I still felt the overwhelming emotions. At one point I wondered whether we would need to get more help than I could provide and explore senior living for my father. I'm the oldest of my siblings and have experience due to my career, so, like Angela, I would be the representative of moving forward with a different living situation for him. I would be taking responsibility for gathering all the information to help make this decision about where our dad would live the rest of his life. Like anyone, I wondered, what if he moves somewhere and it doesn't go well? What if he falls and breaks his hip on day one? What if he's calling my sister twelve times a day because he doesn't want to be there anymore and he feels like I've abandoned him?

The guilt that primary siblings feel is also a very real part of the struggle. Not everyone feels guilty, but that sibling who is doing all the touring, all the questioning and answering at different communities, sifting through decisions, and then having to update the siblings on the options is likely going to also carry the bulk of the guilt. Especially when siblings insist that their Mom or Dad is fine and doesn't need to move anywhere, it's easy to feel like you're the bad guy when you know differently. You are simply working to solve the problem of your elderly mom or dad's living situation. No one wants to do this, but when it becomes clear that you have to do something, then you have to do something.

HIGHLY CHARGED SITUATIONS

The only way to provide them with all this helpful information is to know what the family, and the senior in particular, needs. What is their pain point? What would make a senior living community perfect for them. In short, what are we solving for? We are talking about the place that their beloved parent is likely going to live for the rest of their life.

Not only are these decisions supercharged emotionally, but they are also literally charged—senior living decisions are very expensive decisions. At the time of this writing, a one-bedroom suite in an assisted living community costs anywhere between $5,000 a month in a rural or suburban area to $8,000 a month in a large urban area, with memory care housing in an urban area going up to potentially over $10,000 a month. The bottom line is that this major change, on top of all those emotional costs, and the stress of transitioning a parent out of their own home and into a senior living community, is going to cost families between sixty and 120 thousand dollars a year.

Families are also in the dark about the services, levels of care, and pricing on every aspect of your community, and facing the great unknown is scary. Most families who are looking for senior living don't really understand anything about the industry. Nearly all the individuals who come to this decision are doing it for the first time ever, and while the Internet has made researching senior living and the various types of communities much easier, most people still have next to zero experience with it. They barely know what questions to ask, and it can feel very frightening to think about spending that much money on something you can't fully wrap your brain around.

The way we talk doesn't help. Salespeople in this industry have a bad habit of using too much senior living sales jargon, which depersonalizes the customer's experience. They don't know the difference between AL and IL, for example, and it makes it difficult for them to trust you if you're not speaking in plain English. We need to help our customers understand the information we're giving them by speaking their language, not ours.

Usually all they're worrying about is whether someone is going to answer the call button in the middle of the night. They may be imagining something like a hospital environment or some other experience of healthcare they've had in the past. It's our job to help them see, feel, and understand the benefits of the community that specifically support their biggest concerns, all while educating them on what senior living is and is not. Without this, the customer may be tempted to walk back to the comfort of the uncomfortable current situation.

Additionally, since our customers are usually first-time shoppers and they are about to buy something that will cost them an immense amount of money and profoundly affect their parents' quality of life, the salesperson is a critical piece of that family's decision-making process, and therefore, you have an enormous responsibility. The good news is you also have the opportunity to make a positive contribution to this family's lives.

To do this, you'll need to do the work with as much bravery and vulnerability as you can.

COURAGEOUS CURIOSITY

A long time ago, when I was still a community-based salesperson, I met with a gentleman

named Roger whose mom was living in an independent living community. She received her meals from the community, but she had her own kitchen, and it was more like a little apartment. The community she was living in contacted me and asked me to meet with her and her son because she had been found outside the property wandering around in the streets several times. They thought she might need a higher level of care such as assisted living or memory care.

It was winter here in Cleveland, and there were railroad tracks adjacent to the community, which piled on more urgency to the situation. When I met with the son, I talked to him about the fact that his mother was wandering away from the community and that she might need a different type of care. I went over the facts with him, and his response was, "Yeah, but I don't think she needs to make a change, because she always remembers to put her coat on."

To this day, I can remember saying to him, "Roger, she is crossing the street. She is near the train tracks. She's not letting people know that she wants to go for a walk. Are you sure you don't want us to at least do an assessment to see if this could be a good solution for her? Your mom is wandering away from the community, and it puts her at great risk. She loves to walk and enjoys meeting people along the way. Up to now those people she's met know where she lives and walk with her back to the community. If we work together, Roger, and work with your mom, we can figure out what could be a better living environment."

The end result was not what I was hoping for—Roger moved his mom into his own home, not into our community.

I believe he was just too afraid to make the move that he knew deep down he needed to make. I lost that sale, but regardless, looking back, I know it was the right thing to do.

It took some courage on my part to confront him on what I see now was his own denial. I had to ask courageous questions, hard questions, in my effort to help the family and do my job. Asking courageous questions—and hoping we are asking them at the right time—is a risk we sometimes take, but it's a necessary risk.

While Roger's decision was out of my control, many lost sales are preventable. If you take the time to develop your Curiosity-Driven Sales techniques, you get a lot of that control back, because there is power in building relationships. Building genuine connections with your customers will help you know when the time is right to ask hard questions. Once you get to know your customer, you'll have the instincts and intuition to guide them toward the realization that you are offering the best solution to their problems. But getting to know your customer takes curiosity, patience, and courage.

It takes a lot of courage on the part of families to pick up the phone and talk to a total stranger about moving someone they love into senior living. It also takes a lot of courage on the part of the sales professional to go deep and stay open to feelings like empathy and true curiosity. It helps to keep in mind that these families are putting so much on the line. They have to say things out loud about how their parents are starting to decline, and once they've said it, they can't really avoid the fact that they need to do something about it. That's courageous. As a sales professional, you need to meet their courage with the same level of courage and bravery.

This sometimes means going to the heart of the matter when things get uncomfortable. For instance, you need to be able to ask, "Does your mom go to the bathroom by herself okay?" or "Does your dad still do the things he loves to do?" It takes a lot of bravery to ask a daughter like Angela whether her mom might be avoiding the senior center because she's having trouble getting to the bathroom in time. Angela is going to feel ashamed that she didn't think of that herself, and that makes it a hard question to ask. The moment will be charged with a lot of emotion for both of you.

Just asking one question like that can be a very difficult endeavor. But having the courage and curiosity to ask the hard but necessary questions, really listen to the answer, and follow up with another question that directly pertains to their answer takes double the courage and curiosity. This is why many sales professionals rarely ask a customer more than two or three questions before they jump right into solution selling. Often, they just don't want to go there.

In general, people don't usually look for senior living they think they'll need far in the future. Most of the time it's an urgent situation. However, there are times when it's not urgent, and you might even need to make sure the senior is ready for senior living. Sometimes you have to be the one to help them see that they don't have a hundred-thousand-dollar problem. They might just need to hire some private duty companies to come in and help with laundry and food delivery. You take a big risk asking, "Do you really think it's the right time now?" But as we explore later in the book, anything that builds trust with a customer will help you keep them coming back to you in the long run.

Developing the patience to go a little slower and get to know your customers is a huge opportunity for all salespeople, especially in the senior living industry. That sense of urgency that you feel to close doesn't often lend itself to forming real connections with customers. How can you be one hundred percent engaged with your customer when in the back of your mind you're worrying about whether this person will move in next week? That background noise of trying to hurry the sale and make your numbers this month impairs your listening skills.

Remember, no one wants to do this. Our customers are all just looking for one good reason to walk away. That's why it's so important you master the concepts in the rest of this book—so they will never have a good enough reason to walk away. If you do this right, they will start to feel relief instead of dread. They will realize that they have finally found a place that will actually make things much better for their whole family in the long run.

KNOW WHAT YOU DON'T KNOW

While it may seem counterintuitive, being willing to admit you don't know the answer to a customer's question can increase your chances of closing a sale. Of course, it's vital that you know as much as possible about your community and that you are armed with loads of information and solutions to their problems. We will go over this in great detail later in the book, but for now, consider those times when you truly do not have the answer to a question. In these times, it's important to admit you don't know, find out who does, and bring in their expertise. This can be a very effective strategy for connecting authentically with your customer.

A customer has come to you concerned about their mother's falling. They want to know what your community has to offer in terms of fall prevention and care. You might not actually know the answer to that question, or you might not know the best way to answer it. Should you admit that it's never entirely possible to prevent falls? Or should you dance around that and just discuss potential solutions? While it's tempting to just avoid the question because you don't know, or to give them a vague, generalized answer, it's much more effective to investigate a path toward learning the answer. You probably know who the best person to talk to about this is. Most likely, it's the head nurse of your community. You can talk with them and learn as much as you can, and then you can also arrange for them to meet with and talk to your customer about it when they come for the tour.

If you set up a time for your head nurse to come chat with them about how falls are handled in your community and what measures can be taken to try to prevent them from happening, you can let the customer know they'll be meeting the head nurse when they come. You can say something like, "I hear how important it is to you to make sure that we're the kind of community that will make sure she is least likely to fall, and I think it will be best to talk with our head nurse Irene about it in more depth. I can tell you everything I know we do, but you will love talking to Irene, too, because this is her area of expertise. She can give you a great deal more information about it."

This type of conversation also takes courage, because you are allowing yourself to be vulnerable by admitting you don't know the entire answer. The reason this is a good sales technique is because then you can integrate other people to give the customer as much information as you possibly can so the customer sees that you are setting aside your ego and need to close the sale to be as genuinely helpful as you can.

Let's face it, as salespeople, we have egos. We don't like to be wrong, and most of the time we prefer to look like the surest person in the room. But I would ask you to remember that we're not always going to be right, we're not always going to win, and we're not always going to know the answers.

There are almost always options to investigate a question if something is an issue for a prospective resident and/or their family. That should be part of the planning before the family comes in for the tour. If it's a food issue, you should be talking to the dining team. If it's a medical issue, you can talk with the nurse. Activities-related questions can go to the program director. Be willing to know what you don't know, find out the answer, and learn.

Be brave enough to ask those questions of your staff, too. They are incredibly busy, but keeping you informed so that you can inform your customers is vital to the sales process. It is the only way you can truly demonstrate that you can help solve your customers' problem, build their trust, and get closer to closing the sale.

We've been discussing all the many ways we can help the customer; however, your job is not only to help them. Your job above all is to generate qualified buyers and walk them through a sales process that inevitably leads to them selecting and moving into your community. Unfortunately, many times that job interferes with your ability to give yourself permission to stay the course with your curiosity, vulnerability, and bravery, if you let it. And that is the heart of your struggles.

YOUR STRUGGLES ARE REAL

Senior living sales can be hard on us emotionally because we are dealing with some stressful and sometimes sad situations. But what really makes this so hard for the salesperson is the reality that it's a business. You are expected to produce X number of move-ins per week, per month, per quarter, and per year. Let's say you are expected to get four move-ins a month. You know there will likely be around two move-outs a month. Your goal is to net ten move-ins a year.

That pressure hangs over your head every day. Your supervisor is working under a budget. They have a bottom line. What happens when their bottom line starts to distort your thinking and you feel the need to throw curiosity to the wind and start trying to rush the sale? How do we balance patient, effective, Curiosity-riven Sales with delivering on our metrics?

It's easy to forget that you are taking real-life people through a difficult buying journey. At some point in that buying journey, a care assessment will need to be done to determine what kind of care needs to be provided, how much that care will cost the family, and whether your community can even care for them at all. Of course, this assessment doesn't always happen the first time you meet the family. You might meet with them multiple times, become engaged with them on the phone and in person, showing them all the amazing things their mom or dad will have if they move into your community. You've made calls and had meetings coordinating with your community's caregivers and staff to get the answers you need to do your job well.

All this can sometimes be for nothing, if during the assessment it's discovered that they have a prohibitive health condition and can't live there. Or, more often, you go through all this only to find out that the cost of the room plus the cost of the care needed is completely out of the customer's price range.

By this time, you've invested a lot of time and energy. You've kept them engaged, learned everything you could about them, and kept them moving forward toward the assessment. When the assessment is complete, for the first time, the family has an actual dollar amount. By then, you have jumped through most of the hoops of the buying process. You've dragged them through some difficult conversations, and now they can't even move in. This is one of the many things that makes your job high risk and high emotion for you, the salesperson, too.

You feel your customer's disappointment, but of course, you're also disappointed because you've invested all this time and energy, empathizing with them, going deep, and asking all the hard questions with compassionate, authentic curiosity, only to lose the sale. Your supervisor has been breathing down your neck, and now you're not going to make your numbers. This is hard, especially if you've taken your job seriously along the way and put in a lot of time and effort. So, sadly, maybe the next time, you're not as motivated to put in all the time and effort.

You might spend several weeks getting to know a family and everything about their mom or dad you need to know, but you're still waiting on the assessment before they can decide. Your supervisor comes to you and says, "You know, it seems to me that you've been talking to these people for weeks and having a lot of conversations with them. When are they moving in?"

Suddenly, you feel the pressure to leapfrog in your selling journey over some critical areas that would make it more likely for you to win the sale. Now you are too panicked about getting the move-in to listen deeply to them anymore, and you're going to jump to solution selling. "These are your top five problems we need to solve, and we can solve all five of them. Are you ready to make a deposit?"

The irony is that it's relatively easy to stay aligned with the buyer and their journey, until you are behind the eight ball and need to get that move-in. At that point, the pressure to close the sale undermines your thinking process and your ability to go slow to go fast. Now you can only go fast, and it is likely to backfire. It is likely to cost you the sale.

The best salespeople know how to establish a sense of urgency to hurry the sale without disrupting the relationship-building process, but it's not always possible to preserve that trust if you're rushing. You can't rush this, because you can't rush these families. Often these families are in denial about how quickly they need to decide. They might pick up the phone when you call, but you can't move them forward to the next step for one reason or another. This is when it becomes a battle within you, the salesperson, to balance preserving that authentic relationship with hitting your numbers.

A salesperson who has slowed down to go fast understands the flow of opportunities to move people forward in their decision-making process without pushing too hard. There should be at least some level of pushing them out of their comfort zone, because this is uncomfortable no matter how you slice it. But you can't push them so hard that they hightail it out of your community and never come back.

That's high risk, high emotion. You risk losing a great potential customer because you are no longer aligned with where they are in their buying journey. But at the same time, you have your own high emotion around needing to make this sale.

The many different types of customers you must constantly juggle adds to your pain. You have one group of people you've been working with for a while, and now they really need to decide, so you're at a tipping point with them. It's decision time—will it be us or will it be someone else? And then you have another group of people who are running through your front door, shouting, "My mom's in the hospital, and she's getting discharged tomorrow! I need to figure out what to do!" You also have a third group who are in denial, and at a certain point you have to try to create a sense of urgency to push them forward.

I think of it like soup. The peas and carrots are the people whose parents are in the hospital and being discharged soon, and they need to find senior living right away. The peas and carrots are always in the soup. But the rest of the ingredients, the onions that are not quite ready to get in the pot yet, and the saffron that's too expensive and you can't find at the store anyway, they make the soup difficult to cook. The soup is the balancing act of juggling your different types of families and getting the outcomes you need.

There's a rhythm to everything. Sometimes the rhythm is fast; other times it's very slow. And there's no yardstick to tell you that you can't spend more than twenty hours with one family. There's no time frame. You have to just hang in there and spend as much time as it takes.

You have people who are quick decision-makers, people who are analytical decision-makers, and people who are marinating-in-guilt decision-makers. You have people dealing with their siblings and other people involved. This all makes your work extremely complicated.

Of course, there are sales that are easy. The family is ready, your place is right for them, and they can afford it. But there are just as many if not more that are tough. In many, many cases, you have to balance sales demands with solving the human crisis these families are going through. Everything you do matters at that point: Call them back when you're supposed to. Listen to all they have to say. Meet every person as if it's the first customer you've talked with all day, even if it's Friday at the end of the day.

YOU HAVE AN ENORMOUS RESPONSIBILITY

Professional salespeople prepare for their work. They respect the process. They understand their impact on the process, and they're strategic. The highly emotional aspect of the work comes when they are trying to listen to learn so they can provide tailored recommendations for next steps while staying extremely focused on the outcomes they'll need to make the sale happen.

I believe you have an enormous responsibility as a senior living salesperson. This is where your customers' mother or father will live for the rest of their lives. Day in and day out, you have to show them what your community offers. You have to help them understand the higher cause of giving their parents' dignity and comfort, not to mention happiness, at the end of their lives. You have to get them to let down their guard and set aside their fears and emotions to make the right choice.

If you take your job seriously, then knowing that you are a critical piece of a family's decision-making process is a heavy weight to bear. You have to be at your best for every person that you connect with, regardless of the level of care they're looking for, be it independent living, assisted living, or memory care. Every family will be making decisions based on your recommendations, which come from your authentic curiosity and your willingness to listen to learn as you go. This is your enormous responsibility.

These families are going through one of the most difficult decisions of their lives, and they shouldn't be rushed or hustled into buying a product. They're not all peas and carrots. Many just need to be shown that you care and that you understand their struggle. Only then can they understand that your community offers what they need most: a caring environment. And if you truly have all the little things their loved one needs to be happy, it's your duty to show them that. Our work is tiring, and solution-driven sales make it worse. Solution-driven sales are pretending to be interested, and as I've stated, pretending is exhausting. Genuine curiosity, on the other hand, is not only energizing, it's also quite an effective sales strategy, which is why we need to go slow to go fast.

We already know Edith is a big knitter. She loves to make beanies for babies, and she loves knitting as a way to enjoy time with friends. Her salesperson slowed down enough and took the time to learn this about Edith by asking Angela many personal questions about Edith. She decides to arrange for Edith's tour to be on the same day as her community's Ladies Knitting Circle. The salesperson might say something to Angela about helping her mom wear Depends when she comes, in case there's a wait at the bathroom.

Including the knitting circle on her tour is a big hit. Edith shows the others how she makes the beanies. Edith even makes a couple of new friends. Several days later, Angela calls with more questions, questions her siblings have. She tells her salesperson she's close to making a decision, and within a couple of weeks, Angela is ready to put down a deposit. Going slow to go fast can be just that simple.

THEIR CIRCLE GETS SMALLER

There's a game that we sometimes use to help people understand what happens to a senior as their life gets smaller with age. It's called the yarn exercise, and it is described in detail at the end of this chapter. One person stands in the middle of a circle holding many long pieces of yarn. Everyone else is circled around them, each holding the other end of a piece of yarn, representing an aspect of a senior's life. People take turns answering the question "What are the things that matter in your life?" Maybe they say being a parent, or having great friends, or because I play bridge and love it, or piano and love it. It might be that she's still a swimmer at 83 or that she has a sister and they've traveled a lot. Maybe she was always the driver in her marriage.

Once all of these things are stated aloud by the circle of people, one by one everyone on the outside takes their yarn away from the person in the center, who represents the senior. As they step away one by one, the circle gets smaller. At the end of the exercise, when it's led by an expert, you have someone in the middle just holding two or three strings out of the twenty that were there. This demonstrates the natural loss that happens as we age.

As you age, the strings just go away. You lose friends, loved ones, abilities, and opportunities. You become more lonely and frail, less relevant and fun, and your circle gets smaller.

Don't ever forget that this is such a huge adjustment for prospective residents and their families, way beyond the fact that they won't live at home anymore. Once the customer decides on a place for their elderly parent to move into, they've now defined that parent's circle of friends, how they'll get their meals, what activities they'll experience, what time they'll eat and shower. For anyone in this situation, these are just a few of their concerns. It's only logical that you take the time to develop a genuine interest in your customer and ask meaningful questions.

The flip side of this is that senior living is also an opportunity for seniors to make new friends. Many senior living residents have already lost a lot of their friends by the time they move into a community. Now, in many ways, their world will get bigger. The best salesperson asks the right questions and then listens to learn so they can help them solve their problems and get them through this huge adjustment—so they can enjoy this new bigger life. This is all part of going slow to go fast.

Angela was fortunate to have a salesperson who took the time to be curious and was courageous enough to ask hard questions. But the key to Edith's move-in wasn't only the questions her salesperson asked. It was also what she did with the answers that made the difference. She helped Angela feel seen and heard, and that is what we'll discuss next.

GET CURIOUS (IT TAKES PRACTICE)
UNDERSTANDING LOSSES AND REBUILDING IN SENIOR LIVING

This exercise is designed to help sales professionals empathize with the emotional and social losses that seniors experience as they age and how moving into a senior living community can restore some of what they've lost. By guiding prospective residents to rediscover meaning in a new environment, you can help foster a sense of connection and belonging.

Step 1: Setting the Scene

One person will stand in the center of a circle holding several long pieces of yarn. Each person around the circle should take hold of one end of a piece of yarn. Each yarn represents a meaningful aspect of a senior's life.

Step 2: Identifying What Matters

Go around the circle and ask each person:
"What are the things that matter most in your life?"

Examples might include:

- Being a parent
- Playing a favorite sport like tennis or swimming
- Spending time with lifelong friends
- Traveling with family or a spouse
- Attending religious or social events

As each person shares, they should reflect on why these things are so meaningful. The person in the middle holds onto all the yarn, symbolizing how these important aspects are still connected to their life.

Step 3: Experiencing Loss

Next, ask the people in the circle to imagine what happens as they age and start losing the ability to engage in these important aspects of life. One by one, have participants share what it might look or feel like to lose that ability.

For example:

- "I can no longer drive, so I can't visit my friends whenever I want."
- "My arthritis has gotten worse, so I had to give up playing bridge."
- "I used to travel with my spouse, but they passed away, and now I don't travel."

As each person shares, they let go of their piece of yarn and step away from the circle. The person in the middle will feel the weight of each string falling away, symbolizing how their life gets smaller as they lose these connections.

Step 4: Rebuilding Connections

Now, shift the conversation. Ask the group:

"What question could you ask to help understand what mattered most to this senior?"

For example, you might ask:

• "What do you miss most about playing bridge?"
• "How did traveling with your spouse make you feel?"
• "What aspect of being a parent brings you the most pride?"

Encourage participants to ask open-ended questions that allow the person to share more about their experiences and feelings.

Step 5: Reclaiming Aspects of Life in Senior Living

Finally, ask everyone to brainstorm how moving into a senior living community could help this person regain or re-experience some of what they've lost. Participants should now pick the yarn back up, symbolizing new connections.

For example:

• "You could join our weekly card games where we always welcome new players."
• "We host day trips and have travel groups for residents who love to explore."
• "We have parenting and grandparenting groups where residents share stories about their families."

As the yarn is picked up, the circle gets larger again, symbolizing how the senior can rebuild connections and find new meaning in the community.

This exercise can also be done as an individual exercise with just a few modifications.

This solo version of the exercise will help you build empathy and gain insights into how senior living can restore aspects of life that seniors may have lost over time.

* * *

Step 1: List Important Life Aspects

Start by listing five to ten important aspects of life that might matter most to seniors. Reflect on various categories such as:

- Family relationships
- Social connections
- Hobbies and interests
- Mobility and independence
- Professional or volunteer roles

Write these down in a journal or notebook.

Step 2: Imagine the Loss

Next, visualize how aging might take these aspects away from the senior. Think about what it would feel like to lose the ability to engage in these meaningful areas of life. For example:

- **Family:** "What if I could no longer participate in my family's day-to-day life?"
- **Hobbies:** "What would happen if I could no longer engage in my favorite hobby?"

- **Independence:** "How would I feel if I couldn't leave my house without help?"

Reflect on the emotional impact this might have. Write down your thoughts.

Step 3: Ask Reflective Questions

Think of one question for each of the important aspects you listed that you might ask a senior to better understand what that loss means to them. For example:

- "What did you enjoy most about driving yourself to visit friends?"
- "How did knitting baby hats for charity make you feel?"
- "What was your favorite part of being a teacher?"

This helps you become skilled in asking open-ended, curiosity-driven questions during sales conversations.

Step 4: Identify Solutions in Senior Living

Reflect on how senior living communities can help restore or reconnect seniors with those lost aspects of their life. For each important aspect, think of how your community might provide a solution or support, such as:

- Social groups that bring people together based on hobbies or past professions
- Programming that provides a sense of purpose through volunteer opportunities

- Safe, assisted transportation options that allow seniors to visit friends or participate in outings

Write down your ideas. This step helps you articulate the value of your community during the sales process.

Reflection: This exercise illustrates the profound impact senior living can have by helping seniors reconnect with the meaningful parts of their life. As a sales professional, use curiosity-driven questions to discover what matters most to each prospective resident. Helping them understand how your community can support these important aspects of their life will ultimately make the transition more positive and fulfilling.

Chapter 2

Helping People Feel Seen and Heard

"You were seen, you were heard, and you matter."

—OPRAH WINFREY

Several years ago, during football season, a director of sales in Ohio had been working with a gentleman named Ted and his daughter for quite a while, helping them move forward with his senior living arrangements. It had come to light in their conversations that Ted was a huge Cleveland Browns fan, and by asking a few well-designed questions, the director of sales learned all about his football passion—his jerseys, all of the many, many games he'd been to, and his Browns-emblemed stadium chair and blanket.

In the daily morning meeting that every senior living company has between all of the department coordinators, this salesperson told everyone about this gentleman, because he had finally gotten to the point that he was ready to come in for the tour. That morning, someone on the team came up with an idea:

"Everybody likes football. Why don't we have a football party and invite Ted and his daughter to it?"

Other people chimed in. "Yeah, we have lots of fans here, and we've never planned one before." They went ahead and planned this gathering for the current residents, and when the salesperson was on her next call with him, she was able to share the details of the party.

"I know you love football, and I wanted to let you know the community is having a Monday night football party for all the residents. I know you've been a little hesitant to come in and tour our community, but would you like to come in before the party and then stay for it? We'll have peanuts and hot dogs and beer, and of course the game will be on." Once they agreed to come in, she followed up with, "I'm sure most everyone will be in their jerseys, so don't forget to wear yours."

Just imagine for a moment how Ted felt when she invited him to that, and imagine what he felt when he came in and saw everyone in their jerseys, eating peanuts, drinking beer, and getting ready to watch the game. Imagine how welcomed he felt and how much he had in common with everyone there.

WHAT'S WRONG WITH ASKING WHAT'S WRONG WITH YOU

Had the salesperson only asked the man's daughter something like, "Tell me a little bit about why you called today," rather than asking questions to explore his interests and passions, she might have found out he was having some trouble getting up the stairs and then just continued down that clinical path. I call this kind of thinking and communication with customers the "What bucket are you in?" approach.

I call it the bucket approach because if you're just asking "what's wrong with you" kind of questions, you're just trying to batch people into different buckets based on their problems. You have the "confused and wandering" bucket, the "not taking their medications" bucket, the "can't be home alone because they'll fall" bucket, and on and on. You're missing out on the richness of who they are as whole individuals, with stories, passions, and histories that go far beyond their current challenges. With this kind of thinking, a salesperson is wondering such things as, "How long will it take for you to make a decision? How much money do you have to spend? Will you need memory care?"

If those topics are the focus of your conversations with a customer, you will not reach the kinds of tailored interactions that help people feel seen and heard. You have to go deeper than a "what's wrong with you" kind of question if you really want to stand out in senior living sales.

I can guarantee you that the salesperson who arranged the football party asked more than just those kinds of questions. She didn't ask his daughter something vague such as "Tell me about your dad." Specific details about people can only be learned through specific questions like, "What are some of your dad's favorite things? What kind of guy is he? What does he love to do?"

The key here is to take the time to be genuinely interested in the person, not just their problems, and definitely not just getting the sale. Most people like to talk about themselves, and often you just have to come up with a few initial questions to get them going. When they answer, you just have to listen with genuine interest and ask more questions based on their answers.

You don't need to pepper them with an onslaught of questions. That's not the point at all, and it can backfire and seem insincere. It's not about asking more questions; it's about asking the right thoughtful ones that unlock meaningful insights and human connections. It doesn't really take any more time to dig deep and find the right questions that will get them thinking about things that light them up.

Connecting authentically with people through curiosity helps people feel seen and heard, and that leads to them feeling like they matter. Why is this important? For senior living sales, mattering matters for many reasons.

WHY MATTERING MATTERS

First, you may have the same number of dining room chairs, the same size rooms, and the same activities as the competition, but if only your community has people who genuinely care about solving your customer's problems and giving them an experience that demonstrates they matter, you're dramatically increasing the likelihood they'll move in.

One good question can lead to a lot of information. They might not have been able to tell that story for a long time, or maybe their family hasn't wanted to hear about it again. Give them something back that they hadn't had in a while by being interested. And remember that feeling listened to is a byproduct of mattering.

There is quite a bit of research on mattering in general, mattering in your workplace, and mattering in your relationships, but there is very little research on seniors feeling like they matter. In many cases, seniors are experiencing quite a bit of social isolation and loneliness. They have lost many of their connections with others and the outside world. Many of their friends and relatives have passed away. They aren't always in step with the younger generation, so they feel isolated from the world at large.

Even if they are living with a family member, they can still feel lonely. Their relatives have all heard their stories over and over, and they're tired of them. Deep down they feel like more of a burden to them than the lively, interesting person they once were.

For many people, as you age, you can't drive your car anymore. Many of your friends have died. You might not be able to play cards anymore because of Parkinson's or another affliction. These losses are often unintentionally compounded by family members, who may not even realize how their actions and words deepen the loneliness. Your stories aren't relevant to anyone anymore, your family gets frustrated with you, and it feels like they don't care.

Mattering matters because, for so many seniors, it's been years since they've truly felt valued. I remember speaking with a resident who hadn't had anyone ask about his life story in over a decade, and when we finally did, it brought him such joy. When seniors in that situation suddenly go to a senior living community and feel like they're seen and heard, they're going to innately appreciate that.

As people age, sometimes people tire of listening to your stories. In families, this is especially true. Sometimes seniors experience the feeling of being the obstacle to everyone else having fun. They can't go on vacation because Grandma can't ride in the car for that long or because we can't find someone to take care of Grandma. Your sister can't come to your soccer game because she has to stay with Grandma. This can happen with any family member, be it your kids, your grandkids, or even your spouse.

The memory issues seniors may struggle with make things even worse. People around them can get impatient with their forgetfulness and bored with their repetition of certain things that they don't even remember having said before. For many seniors, it has been a long time since they felt like they mattered. This can lead to depression, which as we know, has all kinds of side effects in and of itself.

But if they decide to join your community, things will look a little different. Their family will be free of the burden of caring for them on a day-to-day basis and will enjoy their company much more. Their peers will be interested in their stories. No one will mind if they repeat themselves; they will have a sense of camaraderie with people of the same age who have so many things in common with each other.

HELPING PROSPECTIVE RESIDENTS FEEL SEEN AND HEARD

So how do we help seniors and their family members feel like they matter? It's not really that
complicated: Find ways to help them feel seen and heard. Leverage your genuine curiosity to help them rediscover their worth, and reaffirm that their stories, experiences, and contributions still hold meaning. You can ask them all sorts of things, but here are a few examples:

- Did they play a sport? Which one? Did they win awards?
- Did they enjoy sewing? (Tip: Perhaps they once crafted a wedding dress or made quilts for family members. Asking about the "why" behind their sewing helps unearth deeper passions.)
- A card player? Which game is their favorite?
- Were they in the military? What was that like?
- What did they do for work? Did they enjoy it?
- What are some of their hobbies? How did they get into that?

Even these seemingly simple questions can spur a senior to look at themselves perhaps a little more objectively and remind them that they have done so many interesting things in their lives, accomplished so much, and enjoyed many different people and places. Ask them everything you can about themselves and then bring out the open-ended follow-up questions based on their answers. These questions not only show that you see and hear them, but they send a deeper message—that their unique journey and contributions still hold significance, even now.

In chapter three, we will explore the technique of using customers' answers to your questions to ask more questions, taking them deeper into the specifics of their experiences and passions. But for now, let's focus on using these strategies to help our customers feel seen and heard so that they feel like they matter.

Let's say a salesperson used these techniques with a woman, let's call her Marge, who used to own a floral shop. Owning that shop was what she did for a living for most of her adulthood. In many communities, fresh flowers decorate the dining room tables, and sometimes the residents will get together and make floral arrangements for other residents who are in the hospital. If that former floral shop owner shares that interest with her salesperson because the salesperson was genuinely curious about her life, then her salesperson might invite her to come on a tour on one of the days that some of the ladies are making centerpieces and floral arrangements.

Now if you're the salesperson, you can introduce her to the group of residents, saying, "Hi, everyone! This is Marge. She loves making flower arrangements just like you all do. In fact, she used to own Marge's Flowers over on Brice Avenue. Does anyone know that place? I thought since she is here for a tour, it might be really fun for her to join you in this activity because she has so much expertise."

LEARN WHAT THEY TRULY CARE ABOUT

Flowers are something Marge really cares about, and when this happens to her, she thinks to herself, *Wow, these people care about flowers, too. There are people here who enjoy the same things that I do. They realize just as much as I do that these flower arrangements are important and that this is meaningful work.*

Getting to know people in this way doesn't necessarily take longer. It's not about asking just any questions but rather thoughtful, intentional ones that show you care about more than just their immediate needs. If you're going to spend thirty minutes on the phone anyway, why not ask questions that uncover who they really are, rather than just focusing on their problems?

It may sound like it will take longer, but if you ask the right questions, the process will actually go more quickly. Asking better questions will make your client feel seen and heard, thus building trust and lowering their guard. It will also save you time in the end, because you're going slow to go fast. As we've seen with Ted the Browns fan and Marge the florist, the knowledge you gain will help you build a solid relationship by helping them experience joy in your community.

Most often in senior living sales, it's the little things we learn and help bring to light in our communities that matter. When we talk about mattering, that's what that means. The little things become big things. And they often lead to improved conversion ratios and more move-ins.

This is not about just pretending to care. You have to actually care. If you're Marge's salesperson, you have to actually want to help Marge feel comfortable and excited about your community. It's not about simply making them feel like they matter—they already do. It's about genuinely seeing and acknowledging their importance in ways that others may have overlooked for years. The fact is they already do matter, no matter what you do. You're not making people feel seen and heard, you're actually seeing and hearing them. You just have to demonstrate it by doing or saying something out of genuine curiosity.

One of the biggest joys of moving into a senior living community, when you do it early enough in a senior's life, is that all of a sudden all of their stories are relevant again. You are living with people who lived through the same era. They've all had different experiences, but they're experiences that no one else they know can relate to as well as their peers can.

When Marge learns from you that she can tour your community on a day when they're making flower arrangements, she's already excited to come for the tour. She may not be excited to move in, but she'll be excited for the flower arranging. Then, once she's there, she meets like-minded people. Similar to Ted and his passion for the Browns, these other ladies in the flower arranging circle are passionate about something that Marge loves. If you think about it, when was the last time this person felt this much of a sense of belonging or relevance? They're engaged in conversation and feeling like they matter. Suddenly they belong to a community of others like them, and their interests are suddenly relevant. They're going to walk away from that feeling much better than they have in a while. Not only is this approach deeply meaningful on a human level, but from a sales perspective, it's incredibly effective at building trust, rapport, and, ultimately, conversions.

Feeling like you don't matter anymore can have serious consequences—loss of appetite, low energy, it can even lead to depression in some cases. Losing some of the things they've cared about can lower the quality of life for many seniors. That's why it's so crucial that we ask these questions and help them remember who they really are and help them feel like they matter.

The bottom line is that the hour Marge spent making centerpieces with other residents while on her tour could very well lead to her moving in. And that will lead to her having the opportunity to make close friendships later in her life and to experience more happiness.

The tailored touches on tours—like setting up a flower-arranging session for a former florist—don't require much effort but can have a profound impact on their decision-making. The hardest thing about orchestrating something like that is just asking enough questions to learn enough to find out something that you can put together for them that will create a more compelling reason for them to come in and tour. If the only thing I learn is that she fell or that he struggles with stairs, how can I create a real connection? I need to know their stories, their passions, and what made them who they are today. Otherwise, there's nothing to build on.

Several years ago, Tina, a community-based salesperson, spoke on the phone with a woman named Belinda. Tina had the wisdom to ask if her mother had been eating okay, and Belinda disclosed that her mother, Mary, hadn't been eating well or regularly enough, and as a result, her medications had been making her sick.

When Mary and Belinda came into the community for the first time, like all visitors, they were taken to the family room. Tina met them there and asked them both if they would like any coffee or pastries. She looked right at Mary, the prospective resident, and asked, "Mary, can we get you a coffee? Would you like a pastry?"

Mary shook her head and just said, "No, I don't want anything."

Tina said, "Okay," and then turned to Belinda. "Can I get you anything?"

Belinda said she would love a coffee, so Tina called the dining room and spoke to the chef, who had been expecting this call, because Tina had primed him for this visit, and they had made a plan. She ordered the coffee, and a few minutes later, the chef came in with the coffee and a pastry tray.

"Hi, Belinda. Here's your coffee," he said. And," he continued, "not to tempt you too much, but these bakery items, we made these this morning. I thought maybe you might like to try them." Belinda took a Danish, but Mary still refused to eat.

"No, no, I just don't really want to eat anything," she said.

So the chef says, "That's fine, I completely understand. But just out of curiosity, if you were hungry, what would you want?"

Mary thought about it for a minute and then said, "Well, I love strawberry ice cream."

The chef then brought her some of his strawberry ice cream and said, "You know, you could taste this. You don't have to eat it all, but I thought you'd just like to try the kind of ice cream we have here." They have a conversation about the ice cream and touch a little bit on her eating habits having changed in recent months. Mary and Belinda were both impressed before they'd even left the family room to tour the community.

Had Tina said, "We have a certified chef and a nutrition program that ensures our residents eat wholesome food every day in line with their medication schedule," the outcome might have been completely different. They might have even yawned a little. But instead, now Belinda was thinking, *My mom matters here.* And Mary was thinking, *I can't believe he took time out of his day to go and do that for me.*

You can guess how that turned out for Tina—Mary moved in just a few months later.

The essence of helping someone feel like they matter is to help them feel seen and heard. Every discussion you have with your customers is important, because every discussion is an opportunity to connect with them and help them feel seen and heard, and like they matter. I consider a tour a success when the customer is able to tell their stories and realizes that here, around others their age and in similar situations, others are interested in what they have to say.

Over the years, I have met countless seniors who have lived extraordinary lives. I have met World War II veterans, champion swimmers, and grandfathers who owned their own successful businesses. If you think about it, most anybody's life has deeply fascinating aspects; your job is to find out what they are.

EVERYTHING YOU DO MATTERS

In later chapters, we will discuss how important your word choice is and other secrets to forming genuine connections during discovery conversations with your customers, but for now, understand the importance of acknowledging the feelings of the family and prospective resident.

Stay mindful of the intense amount of courage it takes to take the step toward senior living. It is incredibly hard for everyone involved. It's never an easy decision. There is always guilt on the part of the family members, and there is always fear on everyone's part that something will go wrong.

Anything you can do to make them a little more relaxed and comfortable can make a huge difference. And everything you do and say matters.

We all have stories, and they are all worth hearing. Learning our customers' stories is part of our jobs. It will help them lower their guard, build trust, and most importantly, raise your chances of closing a sale. Here are some more questions you can ask seniors and their families to help them tell their stories:

- What one thing did they never get to do?
- What are their favorite shows, movies, or music?
- If someone was married for a long time but are now widowed, you could ask:
  ◦ What did your husband do for a living?
  ◦ Where did you get married?
  ◦ How did he ask you to marry him?
  ◦ What is the funniest thing he ever did?
- Get creative with your questions, and don't be afraid to be a Nosy Nellie.

In the June 2023 *Psychology Today* article "Why We Need to Matter to the People Who Matter Most to Us," it was reported that for everyone, mattering is associated with positive relationships, satisfaction, a sense of purpose in life, and protection from social isolation and loneliness. It doesn't feel good to feel dependent and helpless at that age. By helping the woman who had fallen in her room feel like she actually mattered, it affirmed for me that, aside from making money as a senior living salesperson, these kinds of moments are really why we do what we do.

Because it matters.

As a salesperson, you have an opportunity to help people

find their relevance and fun again. Marge has lost her flower shop, but when she moves in, she can start fresh with the community's flower arrangement group. The more genuinely curious you are about the flower shop she owned—asking questions such as "When was your busy season?" or "Did you work on a lot of weddings? or "What's your favorite flower?"— the more she'll see that your community will offer her the kind of joyful lifestyle she hasn't felt in a long time.

The surprising thing is, no matter what conversation follows your questions, just asking the questions is going to give that senior a sense of feeling seen and heard. Just that act tells them that someone cares enough to want to know more about them. Just that act helps them feel more relevant, and it helps them enjoy a few moments reminiscing about their past. Asking these questions is just one example of another principle you need to keep in mind: never forget that everything you do, every word you say, matters. Your actions will shape not just their decision to move in but their entire sense of self-worth during this critical chapter of their life.

You may have the same number of dining room chairs, the same size rooms, and the same activities as the competition, but only your facility has people who genuinely care about solving their problems and giving them an experience of feeling like they matter.

Being genuinely interested enough to help people feel seen and heard really comes down to a simple thing: good manners. It's not rocket science; it's just good manners. But it must be difficult for some of us to ask these kinds of questions because more often than not we don't. If more of us did, we would have one hundred percent occupancy across the board in all senior living communities, and this book wouldn't need to be written.

In a world inundated with information and choices, feeling

seen and heard has become a rare and precious commodity. Taking the time to connect on a personal level communicates to our customers that their well-being is our top priority. This genuine care and attention create a sense of trust that forms the bedrock of a lasting relationship and higher sales numbers.

Making small efforts to help seniors feel like they matter helps you close more sales, and it all begins with the practice of curiosity-driven sales. In the next chapter, we will discuss the importance of asking the right questions and knowing what to do with the answers.

GET CURIOUS (IT TAKES PRACTICE)
UNDERSTANDING THE WHOLE PERSON— CRAFTING INSIGHTFUL QUESTIONS

This exercise will help you prepare to have more meaningful conversations with seniors by exploring different aspects of their life beyond immediate challenges. It is designed to guide you in creating curiosity-driven questions that uncover the whole person—their past, present, and future needs and desires.

Step 1: Draw Six Boxes

Take a piece of paper and draw six boxes. Label them as follows:

1. **Family**
2. **Finances**
3. **Hobbies & Interests**
4. **Spirituality & Religion**
5. **Career**
6. **Care (Medical Needs and Preferences)**

Step 2: Develop Questions

For each box, write down **three to five questions** related to the subject matter that will allow you to learn about the person as a whole, not just their current needs.

Here are some examples to get you started:

- **Family:**
  - Who in your family do you enjoy spending time with the most?
  - What traditions do you and your family celebrate together?
- **Finances:**
  - What are your main priorities when it comes to financial planning for your future care?
  - Have you considered any financial options for senior living that could give you peace of mind?
- **Hobbies & Interests:**
  - What hobbies have brought you the most joy over the years?
  - Are there any new interests you'd like to explore if you had more time or resources?
- **Spirituality & Religion:**
  - How has your spiritual journey evolved over time?
  - What role does faith or spirituality play in your daily life?
- **Career:**
  - What did you enjoy most about your career?
  - How do you stay connected with colleagues or your industry today?
- **Care:**
  - What's important to you when it comes to your health-care and daily care?

○ Have there been any recent changes in your health or care needs that concern you?

Step 3: Collaborate with Your Team

Next, take your list of questions and **share them with others on your team**. Ask your colleagues what additional questions they would ask to gain a deeper understanding of a prospective resident's life. This step helps you expand your range of questions and ensures you're prepared to have thoughtful, engaging conversations.

Step 4: Build Your Pre-Call Plan

Once you have your expanded list of questions, integrate it into your **Pre-Call Plan**. These questions will now serve as the foundation for discovery in your conversations, allowing you to develop deeper connections with your potential residents and their families by understanding what truly matters to them.

By completing this exercise, you'll be better prepared to approach each conversation with a comprehensive understanding of the person you are speaking with. Instead of focusing solely on current challenges, you'll be able to explore their history, values, and passions—helping you build trust and better position your community as the ideal solution.

Chapter 3

Curiosity-Driven Sales

"Much of what I stumbled into by following my curiosity and intuition turned out to be priceless later on."

—STEVE JOBS

I often say that our job, if we do it well, is working with living history. I'll never forget an opportunity I had to meet a woman who truly did make history. Suzanne came to our community with her daughter Lori at a time when they were not in urgent need of finding senior living. They were at the time just planning ahead and exploring their options. Since a significant percent of our move-ins end up being these kinds of long-game customers, I always put just as much time, thought, and energy into the inquiry call, tour, and follow up. This time, my efforts to stay curious paid off for all involved.

When we met in the family room, I couldn't help but notice the tension in the air. I said something like, "I know this is a difficult decision. Please let me know if you have any questions at all."

"Where's the exit?" Suzanne asked and then chuckled.

Then Lori admitted, "Mom doesn't think she's ready for assisted living. She'd prefer independent living. But there have been falls."

I nodded with compassion and tried to stay open-minded. I said something like, "It's not always easy to know which one is best."

As we walked down a residential hallway, I pointed out the shadow boxes all of our residents at Sunrise always had, and I overheard Lori say to her mom, "You could put your diploma in one of those, Mom." Suzanne smiled and nodded.

This was years ago, so I realized Suzanne must have gone to college in the 50s, not a time when many women were attending universities. I asked, "Really? Where did you go to college, Suzanne?"

"She got her PhD from Cornell University," Lori proudly told me.

My jaw dropped. "Wow," I said, "You must have some stories!"

We slowed down and then found a place to sit down for a bit. I asked her what it was like to be a university student back then, and she began to tell me all about it. "There weren't too many gals in my day who went to college," she said. "At first it was a little difficult. But there was one other girl there at the same time, and we became friends. Pretty soon we realized that we were smarter than any of the guys."

We shared a laugh. I was impressed, but I also realized that the conversation we were having was a terrific distraction for them from the challenging task at hand. I went on to ask her more questions about getting that diploma and breaking through the glass ceiling of education.

As our conversation continued, I could feel her becoming

more comfortable, and at the same time, I was truly enjoying learning this fascinating piece of history she had lived.

"You were brave," I said, "to be able to do that during a time when it wasn't the norm."

She beamed and stood a little straighter with pride. Probably for the first time in a while, someone was genuinely interested in her and her story. She felt like her experiences and her knowledge mattered, even to a perfect stranger.

The point is, had I not asked her where she went to school, none of this would have happened. My natural curiosity and ability to engage with her over something completely unrelated to aging or medications, room size or dining options eased her stress. She relaxed and became more open-minded throughout the rest of the tour. I don't think that moment will ever leave me.

I get it. You're in a hurried environment, and there is relentless pressure to schedule more tours and close another sale. The challenge becomes remaining present and curious with your customer in the midst of the whirlwind of demands. You have four other tours coming in and two meetings scheduled for today. But you have to set that aside, be very present, and, yes, stay curious.

If you are able to take advantage of opportunities to learn something about someone, be it on a phone call, a tour, or in a follow-up situation, it will demonstrate that you have an awareness of the value of seniors as whole people. It's not that complicated to demonstrate that. You can just use the tools of curiosity—just look around and notice things and ask questions. It could be something they say, or a necklace someone is wearing, or some other interesting detail about them.

Sometimes the question you ask will open up a whole new door and allow someone, be it a prospective resident or a family member, to share things that they haven't talked about in a while. Maybe no one else had wanted to hear the story of Suzanne's university days anymore, but I did.

If you understand the transformative power of curiosity and how it leads to deeper understanding, tailored interactions, and ultimately, stronger relationships with prospective residents and their families, the results will be more move-ins, regardless of price.

LIVING YOUR BRAND REQUIRES CURIOSITY

We've established that every community offers basically the same five services: tailored care, dining, programming, medication management, and staff training. Additionally, every salesperson has the same three opportunities to demonstrate that their community is the best choice for the customer—the inquiry call, the community visit, and the follow up. The question becomes, how do you stand out from the crowd? The answer lies in identifying what your customer really needs. Whatever lies beyond those five services is always demonstrated through our behavior as it relates to your brand promise.

After you have identified your brand promise, you need to take the time to consider how you can demonstrate that brand promise during the three phases of interaction with your customer. How can you show them what makes you special, not just saying it, but actually doing it? What can you actually do that will differentiate your community?

When we don't differentiate ourselves from the pack, the decision may fall to price, and that's entirely out of our control. But one huge differentiating experience that is entirely in our control is to give the customer our genuine interest.

Demonstrating your brand promise can be done purposefully through curiosity. This means asking specific, sometimes difficult and sensitive questions. You ask these questions to help gain the knowledge that will allow you to demonstrate what your community offers in a way that is tailored to the customer's needs. You can only "live your brand" effectively in a sales situation if you know enough about your customer to show them, not sell them, the ways in which your community can address those needs and how you can help solve their problems.

Armed with a wealth of knowledge gained through genuine curiosity, your interactions become more meaningful and tailored. Rather than offering generic solutions, you can now present options that align precisely with the unique preferences and requirements of each prospective resident and their family. This tailored approach not only increases the likelihood of a sale, but it also sets the tone for the exceptional experience they can expect within your community once they move in.

During discovery, you should be asking questions that help you learn which staff should also meet with them on the tour so that you can be strategically collaborative with the other staff in the community to demonstrate your brand on the tour. In the previous chapter's example with Mary and Belinda and the strawberry ice cream, their salesperson, Tina, had planned it all out with the chef, down to the smallest details.

If, through your curiosity, you discover that the gentleman you are giving a tour to is on a vegan diet, and your community typically sends out cookies that are not vegan after a tour, go the extra mile. Find a place near you that sells vegan cookies and send him those instead. He'll be moved by your thoughtfulness, and this small act will become a differentiator. Even better, ask your chef if they will make a batch of vegan cookies.

The chef can even share with the prospective resident that they took it on as a challenge and want to know how their cookies stack up against the customer's favorite store bought cookies. Now that would make an impression!

Living your brand is another way of saying that you've aligned the experience of being in your community with what people have seen on your website during their research. When they come in, they see the connections between their initial research, and this builds their trust in you.

THE RIGHT QUESTIONS

Curiosity may not come naturally to most people, including me, but it is a skill that can be developed. There is a lot more that goes into Curiosity-Driven Sales than just wanting to know something. Designing the kinds of questions that will lead you to knowledge you can use in the sales process is essential in getting your curiosity to pay off.

Before we get to strategies for asking better questions, let's take a look at what might be considered the traditional questions.

There are always going to be questions we ask aimed at getting the specifics of a current situation. We do want to know what the current living situation is like, what the challenges are to that arrangement, and what drove the prospective resident and family to start their search. These are important questions, but we need to go beyond the information the customer already knows. I mean, it's their situation, so they likely understand it pretty well. These questions help us, not them. Necessary? Yes. Stopping there? No.

You don't need to ask how old their mom is. She's old; that's why they're looking at senior living. You don't need to know what's wrong with her on the superficial, obvious level. That gets you nowhere. Something is wrong, obviously, or she wouldn't need to find senior living.

A better question might sound something like, "What does your mom's day look like right now?" or "On a good day, what are her routines?" You can also ask if the senior is living alone in their own home right now, and if so, you can ask how that is going. These questions help you go slow to go fast, because you will learn a lot from that conversation that you can use in the sales process.

QUESTIONS THAT OPEN DOORS

Think of it as having a normal conversation with a friend or the mother of a friend. You just naturally make an effort to have a balanced conversation about a variety of things. What do you like to do for fun? What are some of your favorite foods? All of these types of questions are open-ended rather than closed-ended.

Open-ended questions can lead to much richer discovery than closed-ended questions, which only require a "yes" or a "no."

For instance, if you ask them if their mom likes to garden (yes or no), they'll tell you either she does or she doesn't like to garden. But if you ask her what her hobbies are, they might say bird watching, and then you can help them find a room with a good view out to an area where a lot of birds usually fly and where a bird feeder could easily be installed near her window.

Closed-ended questions shut down our ability to learn about our customers. They funnel people in a very specific direction, whereas open-ended questions give people the option to go in any direction they need to in order to talk about their particular situation.

Sometimes it's the little things that lead to valuable answers. "Does your mom (or dad) like to cook?" can lead to "What does she like to cook?" and that can lead to "My mom makes the best chocolate chip cookies," which gives you the opportunity to say, "Well, our chef makes some great ones too; maybe when you come for the tour, you two could have a bake off!"

Closed-ended questions are often super specific questions about their physical condition or other common circumstances of aging, such as:

- How many meals a day are you eating?
- How long have your knees been bothering you?
- Are you on a special diet of any kind?

They know all the answers to those questions, and so it doesn't stimulate them to think about their real problems—the thing or things that warrant a $100,000 annual solution. The same goes for asking them if they are concerned about a particular issue or afraid of any negative consequences of their father's hip problems.

This kind of curiosity is not valuable for the customer. Instead, ask them questions they maybe hadn't even asked themselves yet.

If you ask whether she worked outside the home, you might learn she ran a bed and breakfast for thirty years. This gives you an opportunity to ask things like, "What was that like? Did you meet a lot of interesting people? What kinds of things did you serve for breakfast?" Suddenly you have a fountain of information. If she says, "Oh, our house specialty was our cinnamon rolls," you can talk to the chef about making some or ask her to bring in her recipe for the chef to try if she's willing to share it.

Always keep in mind that this is not the grand inquisition. The dangers of your inquiries ending up feeling like an inquisition are real, and at that point, you're operating under the law of diminishing returns. There's a time to get curious, and there's a time to get off the curiosity bus.

How much curiosity is too much curiosity? When is curiosity not the right approach to take? Some of this comes with developing your instincts over time and paying attention to the nagging feeling that it is time to give recommendations, rather than ask questions, because let's face it, that's what people are coming to you for. But your recommendations should be based on the things you've learned through your curiosity.

Timing is also a factor in this. If someone is in the hospital right now, and the family is in an urgent situation, scrambling to decide what to do next, you don't want to ask them about their hobbies—that would clearly be inappropriate. This would be a good time to ask only the pertinent questions and to make recommendations where it seems sensible to do so.

You also need to beware of offering a solution to their problem too early. It takes time to build up the value of any particular solution. First you need to build a relationship and a solid understanding of their situation and their needs. Perhaps a customer calls and says, "My mom has been acting confused." All of a sudden you are excited because now you can tell them all about the memory care neighborhood in your community. The problem is that in jumping right to that, you've missed out on a thousand other things that are going on with her that may be significantly more important.

In this case, because you were listening to reply and listening to solve, you made a move way too early to provide them with a solution for something that the family probably hadn't even thought through yet. All those extremely well-crafted questions that are based on the answer to the last question you asked them are what will build up the value of your solution.

BUILD PYRAMIDS

If you're curious but you don't do anything with that information, then that's purposeless curiosity. You didn't take those raw ingredients and bake them into a delicious cake of experiences that demonstrate everything you have to offer and move the sale forward. One way to do that is to do what I call building pyramids.

Imagine you're having a conversation with a customer, and every time they share a problem they're having with you that you want to delve into and help them solve, that problem is a little box, like: Mom's not taking her medication. You gather that information and put that box aside, and you keep talking to them and learn she also hasn't been eating very well. Now you have a second box called Poor Nutrition. You put that little box aside, and then you hear from the daughter that she is bringing over her mom's meals herself and putting them in the fridge with dates on them so they don't expire.

The daughter shares how hard that's been to keep up with now that it's soccer season, and that becomes another box, Daughter's Conflicts with Parenting. Eventually, you can carefully stack all of those boxes, and your curiosity-driven conversation is going to give you a pyramid of things that you can effectively use to demonstrate to your customer that your community will help with all those things. This is the difference between solution-based selling and curiosity-driven selling.

If you were practicing solution-driven selling, you would be staying focused on the very first problem you learned about and not letting the boxes pile up. Instead, you were just going to push a solution for that one thing. It costs the same amount of money as what solving their pyramid of problems would cost them, except they are only getting one of their boxes solved.

If that box doesn't happen to be a really big ticket problem, then you as the salesperson will be facing a lot of obstacles to the sale. You'll have to spend a lot of time overcoming those obstacles, all because you didn't spend the time to listen and really try to unearth all of the problems until there was a big pile of them in front of you and your customer, a tsunami of problems coming at the both of you that need to be solved.

If you have that pyramid of boxes, that tsunami of problems, then you are better able to have a deeper conversation and share with them what you've taken in. You'll be able to reflect that back to them to see if you've heard all of it, to see if there's anything else. You would ask them if what you understand to be the problems resonates with what they feel are the problems. This sounds like, "Here are the five or seven things I'm hearing you're dealing with." Then you can ask, "Do you feel like we've covered everything? Are there some things you're more worried about than others?"

This leads to a conversation about everything the customer has told you so far, rather than a conversation about the fact that their mom isn't taking her medications on time. If it is just about the medications, you can tell them that your community has a medication management program and that will solve their problems. But then they might come back and say, "You know, we are going to just try using a pill pack for a while and put some reminders on her fridge, so I don't think we need to pay $100,000 a year after all."

It sounds really sweet and nice when you are having this in-depth conversation about all of their different issues and problems, because you're setting aside your sales goals to really get to know this person, and you genuinely want to understand everything about them you can. And it is really sweet and nice. But the great news is that it's also extremely effective! From taking all this time with them, you're going to get an avalanche of information, not just a couple of issues that need to be addressed, and that avalanche is going to lead to a move-in.

The idea of building that pyramid is really just a way to conceptualize how you can

demonstrate your understanding of the complexity of the situation and the various stressors on your customer. Solution-based selling, similar to the "what bucket are you in" mentality, reduces the person down to just one or two problems. That is just minimizing the enormity of the situation and the enormity of your responsibility to help your customers.

This is also another example of the concept of slowing down to go faster. Have deeper, more robust conversations. What you talk about sometimes might not always be pertinent to you closing the sale. You're simply working to better understand the customer, which will then allow you to catapult them forward when you do get down to prioritizing what is most important to them.

If you're speaking with the family, this includes discussions around things like how the senior feels about moving in, whether they know you're considering senior living, and how you, the salesperson, can help them prepare for those conversations with their loved one. You may have the same number of dining room chairs, the same size rooms, and the same activities as the competition, but if only your community has people who genuinely care about solving many of their problems and helping them feel like they matter, your community is going to stand out.

It all comes down to treating people for the totality of who they are. Armed with the pyramid, you can engage your entire team in the first tour, and the tour demonstrates that you can solve all of these problems. But only because you know what those problems are, and that is only because you were curious and patient.

You will often find that you need to resist the urge to solution sell. Just keep telling yourself: The More I Know, the More I Close. It's a lot harder for a family to walk away from seven problems than it is for them to walk away from one.

When you feel the urge to solve the first problem they mention, don't. Just continue to question. After all, this is an extremely expensive sale, and their problem has to be extensive enough to warrant the cost. The only way to learn the extent of their problems is to be genuinely curious.

HIDDEN TREASURE

After you do all of that discovery, you are going to summarize for the person everything you've heard, and you are going to ask if there are any pieces still missing. And most often that missing piece is the worst problem of all.

A conversation might go something like this: A salesperson says, "I've taken some notes as we've been talking today, and I want to make sure I didn't miss anything. It sounds like you're saying you have five things you're really worried about." And the salesperson repeats back the five things in a way that shows they have really integrated it. And then they might say, "Do I have that right?"

The customer then says something like, "You know what? I guess we didn't talk at all about the fact that she fell in the shower and almost broke her hip."

They talk about that for a few minutes, and the salesperson says, "So now we have the five main issues, and we had better add that she's not always stable on her feet. Of all those things, which one are you most concerned about?"

And the customer says, "Well, actually, I'm most concerned about the fall. It's kind of weird I didn't mention that when we first started talking." And the salesperson says, "No problem at all. I can understand why that would be important to you, and rather scary."

The truth is it's not weird. It's human nature. And often it takes that extra time to get there, because in these situations, it's human nature to minimize the worst parts of a problem. People want to avoid talking about that at all costs, and so they've minimized it in their minds, and that's exactly why the customer forgot about the fall in the shower.

The bigger the problem is, the longer it takes somebody to say it out loud. They have a mental block on it, and now you've gotten it out of them and reflected it back to them. And now, as opposed to thirty minutes earlier, you have uncovered a hundred-thousand-dollar problem.

You have just built a pyramid of little boxes with a bunch of problems, and you've reflected those back to the customer. It becomes difficult to just walk away from these problems and not want them fixed after you've heard them spoken out loud. Then, by summarizing what you've heard and confirming that that is everything—and getting them to say, yes, that's everything, or even better, no, there's one more thing, and it's the worst of all—everything really sinks in.

They realize how serious their situation is, because they have just had to describe all the things that have been weighing on them. From a sales methodology perspective, that's purposeful because, since this is a very expensive sale, what you're solving for has to be worth the money. One little problem is likely not worth a hundred thousand dollars a year.

This is a powerful, highly effective sales approach. And it takes relating to them in an authentic, human-to-human way every step of the process. This lowers their guard bit by bit, and pretty soon they are telling you everything they know. They don't always know everything, and there are often surprises that arise in the assessment, but you get close.

BE CREATIVE IN YOUR CURIOSITY

Creativity probably isn't the first thing that comes to mind when you think about senior living sales strategies. You're not going to play an instrument or paint a portrait. You don't always get to use your creativity on a daily basis.

However, where creativity can truly flourish for salespeople is through curiosity. In fact, you need to be creative to perform in Curiosity-Driven Sales. Because suddenly you are in control of what questions you ask, and you are in control of how you ask them.

You will find a way to ask the questions that fit with your nature, be it academic, jokey (like yours truly), analytical, or whatever your communication style. This will be explored in more depth in the chapter on authenticity, but here we are talking about dialing up your ability to ask good, maybe even great questions. That is where you want to put your energy. I like to say that the only way you can really differentiate yourselves is through behavior that is sustainable. And curiosity-driven genuine connections formed through creative thinking are definitely that.

Let's say you have ten families in the very early stages of the buying process. You're not closing any of them this month.

However, you have a better likelihood of closing them eventually if you really invest the time. It's not even the time you invest; it's the work of asking the right questions. Ask yourself, "What do I need to learn? How can I learn those things in order to help me to recommend what the next step should be for them? How can I think differently about this situation and ask questions that are unique?"

DIFFICULT QUESTIONS

It's great to ask a lot of questions. It's great to listen really well. It's great to do all these things, but if you don't build rapport that allows you to ask the difficult questions or give the difficult recommendations, you won't get far.

If a customer tells you that her dad has been found over at the neighbor's three times this week. and you choose not to go there simply because the customer doesn't seem to think it's a big deal, then you're avoiding an opportunity to ask a hard but vital question. How often does their dad leave the house unattended? Has he ever wandered farther than the neighbors? You're the professional, and you have a responsibility in this space to ask these hard questions, for the good of the whole family. If all of these little missed opportunities add up to the customer deciding not to try to move their senior, that would be the worst outcome.

Some of the more difficult topics you might find yourself discussing include wandering, hygiene issues such as incontinence, medications, and forgetfulness. All of these have in some way aspects that are "taboo" to talk about and can take a lot of bravery on the part of the salesperson as well as courage on the part of the customer to have a discussion about them.

Often, you need to include the department experts at your

community in these difficult conversations. A daughter who is dealing with her mom or dad taking either too much or too little of a medication should share that with the salesperson, but it can be a touchy subject. If the salesperson doesn't ask about how well they're doing taking their medications, it might not come up. Issues with pills can be tricky because it's a hot-button issue.

In advance of this, the salesperson should be chatting with their head of nursing care or a wellness nurse. That should be the salesperson's first conversation—sharing what she's learned in her discovery about medication habits and seeing if there is more research that can be done. Maybe they are coming in for the visit at two o'clock, and so you ask the nurse what time would be best for the customer to meet with them. The nurse will then have time to prepare for the discussion and draw up their own list of questions.

You as the salesperson need to refrain from making any specialized medical recommendations, especially if they might be contradictory to anything their doctor has said. You don't want to assume any diagnoses, and this is why it's crucial to have a medical professional in on this part of the conversation. After you say something like, "I know when we talked about some of the medication issues, I could tell that those were really weighing heavily on your mind. I thought it would be best if our head nurse came in to talk with you a little bit today. She might be able to put your mind at ease or at least give you some questions you might want to ask their doctor."

The nurse then comes in and does the heavy lifting, asking how long they've been on the medication, how many times a day they take it, what time of day, and if they're skipping doses. She would help figure out what's getting in the way. She would explore the connection between the senior's appetite and their medications. The nurse might have many more suggestions, such as working with their doctor and timing the dispensing of the medication properly around meals, and explaining how this will all integrate into their tailored care plan.

Partnering with your medical staff for sensitive health issues adds a more professional and clinical lens on uncomfortable topics, and that professionalism raises the credibility of your whole community, as opposed to just explaining that the company trains your care team really well.

It's still about asking difficult questions to uncover what's really going on, but in this case, you the salesperson become more of a bridge between the caregiver and the family. As the salesperson, you're mainly just stepping back and listening. But once that care professional leaves the room, you will continue to follow up. Don't just let that conversation go in one ear and out the other. Continue to integrate that information as you build your relationship. It's like saying, "I'll make sure they have plenty of strawberry ice cream on hand," after learning it's Mary's favorite food.

In the instance of the medication dosage, you might say, "You will love our wellness nurse Sandy, who you just met. She is really great with helping people manage their medications and really funny, too. Everybody loves her."

Through this process, you are building a story with this family, of their needs and how you will address them. And one would hope, if you have found yourself in the senior living business, that you actually have some interest in older people. If this isn't the case, you might want to reconsider this line of work. It is not a sexy sales career. But it is one that matters a lot.

From a sales process perspective, when you're on that hamster wheel, and you're just trying to catch the things that are flying by you, as opposed to having the opportunity to have more meaningful conversations with a broader spectrum of people in your lead base, your job is a whole lot more interesting. You now get to have good conversations with people. You also are likely providing another human being an opportunity to know that they matter, and that can feel great.

If you can't do that, if a family visits four senior living communities, and no one goes beyond "Can you afford us?" and "What's wrong with you?" and "How quickly can you move in?" then they will make a choice based on price and location, which are important, of course, but we are talking about the way someone is going to live the rest of their life. When you miss the opportunity to really tie what you have to what they need beyond just food and medication, you are denying them an opportunity to live their best life.

It takes a certain amount of discipline to stay in the moment and remain genuinely curious. It takes discipline because you've got four other families that you're supposed to call back when you get off this call. You need to be in the right frame of mind to ask questions that are not solely about what's wrong with them.

When I talk about Curiosity-Driven Sales, I talk about all these things. It's a lot more fun. It's living history. You get to acknowledge a person in the way that they know they matter. And above all, the more you know, the more you close. The work of Curiosity-Driven Sales is to build up a vault of knowledge about an individual that will help you tie what they need to what your community offers. It allows you to know people are going to say things to you that they weren't even thinking about, which is going to give you an opportunity to demonstrate something to them that no one else will demonstrate.

Your job is more interesting when you're curious, but it is not always easy. Because, let's face it, sometimes you're not all that curious. Sometimes you might not be able to muster up enough genuine curiosity. It's a skill, however, that will help you learn more than your competitors about your customer. And if you can learn more, you're going to be able to tie more of the things that you do to what they need, which will increase the value of your offering. It's as simple, and as challenging, as that.

Curiosity is the cornerstone of the slow down to go faster philosophy. It's not about extracting information for the sake of a sale but about truly understanding the unique needs, preferences, and concerns of each individual. By asking open-ended questions and actively listening, we signal to our prospective residents and their families that their experiences and desires are valued.

It takes discipline to be in the moment and be curious, but it's also an act of generosity, and that feels good. And since the more you know, the more you close, it is worth your while to discover what their real problem is. Is it big enough to warrant this extremely expensive sale? Deep discovery pulls you in, as if you're watching a good movie or reading a good book, and before you know it, your job has gotten a lot more interesting, one meaningful interaction at a time.

Suzanne's achievements at Princeton are remarkable, but in reality, most everyone has a remarkable story from some point in their life. If you can think of your work as pulling those stories out of people during discovery periods, it will make your job a whole lot more effective, not to mention fun.

Of course it's not enough to just be curious and get your avalanche of information. You'll also need to know how to use that information to demonstrate your brand in your interactions with the customer. And the next step in that process is to sharpen your listening skills so that you gain as much knowledge as possible about their unique situation. Continuing to question when you feel the urge to solve isn't easy. It's about patience, and it goes hand in hand with listening to learn.

GET CURIOUS (IT TAKES PRACTICE)
BUILDING YOUR CURIOSITY MUSCLES
Step 1: Reflect on Your Comfort Zone

Before diving into curiosity-building exercises, take a moment to **reflect** on where you stand. Ask yourself:

- Are you resistant to becoming more curious or empathetic in your interactions?
- Do you feel like you know enough, or are you open to learning more about others' experiences?
- What can you do to be more naturally inquisitive in your conversations?

Write down some ideas that come to mind. Perhaps you need to practice asking better questions, actively listen, or take time to read more diverse perspectives. This self-assessment will help you identify areas where you can expand your curiosity.

Step 2: Play the "Twenty Questions" Game

Now that you've reflected, it's time to put your curiosity into action through a **role-playing exercise.**

Instructions:

1. **Partner up** with someone for this activity.

2. One person writes **four personal challenges or problems** about themselves on an index card. These challenges could be minor or deeply personal. On the same card, they also write down **four additional things** about themselves that haven't been revealed.

3. The first person **shares only the initial four problems** with their partner.

4. The partner now has **two minutes** to ask questions about the first four problems. The goal is to dig deeper and uncover the other four undisclosed challenges or facts.

   ◦ The second person should focus on asking **open-ended questions** that get the first person to reflect more deeply on what they're sharing.

   ◦ As the conversation evolves, try to pick up on hints, body language, or emotions to figure out if there are deeper, more serious issues behind what's been initially shared.

5. Once the two minutes are up, see how many of the hidden challenges were uncovered through questioning.

The goal is to enhance your ability to go beyond surface-level information by fostering empathy and curiosity in a conversation. The more you practice asking open, thoughtful questions, the better you'll be at unearthing deeper insights and connecting with others on a meaningful level.

This exercise will help build the curiosity "muscles" needed to better understand your prospects' true needs and motivations.

Chapter 4

Listening to Learn

"The art of conversation lies in listening."

—MALCOLM FORBES

During an assessment, Sally looked over Edith's medical records and noticed something was a little off. Curious, she formed a well-phrased question.

"Edith, it looks like you've lost a lot of weight recently. Can you tell me a little bit about the kinds of meals you prepare for yourself?

Edith replied, "I have a meal delivery service, but I don't really like the stuff that people bring me."

Sally let this sink in. From that one open-ended question, Sally had just learned several important things. Edith obviously couldn't cook for herself if others were bringing her food. Edith was particular about what she would eat. And Edith's appetite was most likely diminished, possibly due to medications. The lack of normal eating habits could also be affecting her ability to take medications that require food.

As salespeople, we can learn a ton from listening carefully

to the answers to just one socially driven question. The key is to always listen thoughtfully.

Abraham Maslow's expression "To a man with a hammer, everything looks like a nail" tells us that if you only have one tool in your toolbox, you are only going to be able to fix things that tool can fix. This applies here to our work in the discovery phase with a customer because we often just use solution selling to try to fix the first thing they mention. But if we ask the open-ended questions we discussed in the last chapter, we'll get loads of information, and this gives us loads of tools we can use to solve multiple problems.

It's helpful to think about the difference between listening to share what you know and listening to truly understand. True intentional empathetic listening, and being interested in the answers, gives you the knowledge you need to take your customer's situation seriously and help them see that your community can address those concerns and needs.

Put another way, when we talk about listening to learn, we are talking about the difference between listening to truly understand a person's situation and listening for an opportunity to share what you have to offer. What can be confusing for sales professionals is that to do our jobs well, we need to listen to determine whether we are a good fit for this customer or not. However, if you are just sitting there anxiously waiting to hear some buzzword that will give you the opportunity to "feature dump" everything you have at your community, you are missing the opportunity to know more and, ultimately, to close more.

In true Curiosity-Driven Sales, you want to understand as much as possible about the customer more for the sake of just wanting to understand that person versus for the sake of a sale. For example, if a customer says, "My mom forgets where her car keys are a lot." And then you say, "Oh, we have a great memory care neighborhood," then you are not listening to learn as much as you are listening to offer a solution. You're a victim of the buzzword.

This kind of derailment of your listening skills happens when all we are trying to do is tee up reasons to tell the customer what our community offers. Of course we are going to do that as well. But when you're not listening with a curious ear, and you're not genuinely trying to learn about this person and the challenges that they might be having, you as the salesperson are going to miss out on discovering why your very expensive solution could be the right solution for their problem. You'll be presenting features that don't have the value that equates to your product, because you haven't found all the problems that they need solved. It takes discipline to stay focused on a customer's whole story, but that discipline will be rewarded with more sales.

Listening is a discipline most of us have lost in this day and age. Instead, we want to talk about how beautiful our community is. We want to tell them that if they just come in and meet everyone and see the building, they'll understand what a great place to be it is. But your job is really to stay in tune with that person so that hopefully you can uncover something really important you can help them with. And your job is to do this because you're genuinely interested in what this person is saying. You genuinely want to understand the problem and understand why it's a problem.

Aside from just being receptive and listening, how do we find all the problems that need to be solved? How do we find their most serious concerns? What strategies can you use to steer your customers in the direction of revealing what their real problems are? Let's explore some approaches.

FROM THE VERY FIRST CALL

It starts from the very first words of the very first conversation. Someone calls to get information about your community. You say, "Terrific. My role here is to help families and prospective residents better understand senior living and how we may be able to support you. Can I ask whether you are calling for yourself or for a family member?"

They tell you they are calling for their mom or dad. Then it's your opportunity to ask if you can talk with them a little so you can better understand their situation. "Is there anything top of mind that you wanted to understand or learn more about when you picked up the phone to call us?"

They will probably say something like, "Yes, I need to know how much it costs. Also, I'm not sure it's even what my mom needs."

At that point you can tell them that those are two really important questions. And you can ask them if you can learn a little bit more so you can give them the information they need to make some decisions. They say, "Sure." This gives you the opening to ask some open-ended questions, like "Tell me a little bit about what's going on with your mom right now that provoked you to call today?" or simply "Can you tell me a little bit about what's going on?"

If they say something like, "Well, my mom lives alone. She called me three times last night wondering why I wasn't home from school yet. That was very unusual behavior for my mom, so we took her to the doctor this morning."

To get them to keep going, you might want to say something like, "Okay. What did you find out?"

"They're testing her for a UTI, because they said oftentimes a UTI can cause this kind of new confusion. But the experience really worried me."

Your response might be "I can understand why you'd be worried about that. Has your mom exhibited any other signs of memory loss?"

"Well, she's forgetful, but certainly not to that degree before this. That was a pretty big departure from what we've been dealing with."

"It sounds like in the past you hadn't been very concerned about her staying by herself."

"Right. That really wasn't an issue."

"Okay, let's talk about this a little bit more. In the normal course of a day, what kinds of things does your mom generally do? What does her day look like?"

"Well, I know she doesn't always eat breakfast. In fact, I'm bringing over food for her every week because sometimes she won't even eat until later in the day. So I've been trying to bring some things over to her so she'll at least get something in her stomach before she has to take her morning medications."

"Oh, good. Are you finding that she's been eating what you've been bringing her?"

"I think so. I was really kind of worried about the medications because I know those upset her stomach if she eats them without food."

"Right. Have you noticed whether there have been days that she hasn't taken her medications?"

"I'm not really sure about that. She complains that one of them makes her sick to her stomach, which is why I thought if I brought her over something, that would help with that. But, you know, now that you ask, I guess I'm not really sure about the medications."

"Okay, well, that's fine. That's something you can check into and talk to her doctor about as well."

And on and on it goes, just like a normal conversation.

This is the key: you're asking questions based on the answers they give you. Everything is just a follow up of some kind, and usually it's a request for more clarification or explanation.

But too often in that situation what happens is more like this:

The customer says, "So, I took my mom to the doctor this morning. They think she probably has a UTI. She was really confused last night."

If the salesperson is thinking only about how they can build up to the fact that coming in for a tour or taking some kind of next step is the most important thing, they say, "Well, it's great that you're starting to look into senior living today. I think that probably the next best thing to do would be to get you in for a tour."

One of the problems with this kind of response is that, even if they're ready for a tour, you aren't ready for the tour, because after talking to the customer, you don't know anything that would help you cater that tour to this particular person. All you know is that their Mom was confused and might have a UTI.

When you're listening to learn, it will sound much more like the first example than the second. The second example is really just listening for a buzzword like "confused" so you can show them the memory care neighborhood. I can think of a thousand better ways to conduct that conversation, and they all involve caring more about the details.

First and foremost, we want to recommend the next step to them that makes the most sense. Secondly, we want to ensure that if the tour is the next step we recommend, we can create an experience for them that will show them what life will be like if they move in. Thirdly, we want that tour experience to be a differentiator between ourselves and the competitor.

If all we know is that she might have a UTI, we will discuss how we could help with that through nursing care. But guess what? Your competitor is going to talk about that same thing. There's no value add, no differentiator. Your genuine curiosity is the differentiator.

Especially in the cases where your community will cost the customer a thousand dollars a month more than your competitor, if you're doing the same thing for a medical situation that everyone else is doing, it doesn't warrant the cost. The only thing that really can warrant the cost is if you make them feel seen and heard by asking enough questions and being genuinely interested.

If you're asking to solve, you're not asking to learn. And you won't be able to support that person with anything else that matters other than the one thing you just learned. And this is where the saying "Every man with a hammer is looking for a nail" applies. You are just looking for a nail, rather than a whole building, or in this case, a whole person.

Feeling like you care about them as a whole person will matter to the customer. You need to be able to prepare for the tour and other future interactions, and you can't do that in a way that will make them feel seen and heard unless you really listen with genuine curiosity and a desire to learn.

Odds are, if this is the first time their mom has been confused, it probably is a UTI. This is an acute situation, but it's not chronic. The doctor will treat their mother with antibiotics, and everything will be fine again. That alone doesn't warrant senior living. But in the above situation, the salesperson discovered that there is something else going on. Their mother is not reliably taking her medication, and she's not reliably eating breakfast. Those discoveries came from a salesperson listening carefully while still remaining aware of their sales strategy, which is to learn things that point to this person's needs that might tie into what the community offers.

Staying aware of why you are listening (to learn and to sell!) helps you be more effective as a salesperson. You are trying to understand the next steps for them, whether they need to see a doctor and take antibiotics and that's it, or they need to get in your funnel and schedule a tour.

If somebody says their mom or dad is confused, you need to fight the urge to say, "Well, the good news is we have a secure memory care neighborhood that serves people who are living with dementia." That's a lovely thing to say. It's fantastic. But if all you know is that their mom or dad is confused sometimes, and you simply tell them about your memory care neighborhood, they will not feel like you actually care. They'll hear those words and intuitively know you are just trying to make your numbers.

THE TREASURE CHEST

Think of all the really important information that you are trying to learn as a buried treasure chest. You can be curious in a way that is like taking a shovel and digging a hole that is deep in the ground and finding the treasure chest of information. You found it because you went deeper and deeper into the conversation by putting your shovel in the ground again and again in the same place. Or you can be curious without listening to learn and just keep digging shallow holes all over the place. You're in one spot first—call it memory care. Then you run over a little ways and put your shovel in another area—call it nutrition, and you find a little nugget about her skipping breakfast, and then you run over to the falling area and dig again and find another nugget that she has had some falls. You still have to put the shovel in the ground the same number of times, but this way you get the opportunity to talk about the advantages and benefits of your community.

The problem with this is you're never going to find the treasure chest of information that has the hundred-thousand-dollar price tag on it because you're just asking surface questions and then moving on. You're gathering little nuggets instead of digging out the treasure chest. Listening to learn is like taking the shovel and digging deeply in one place before moving on.

If you're digging really deep, you find the treasure chest that opens up and leads to them realizing they should come in for a tour.

Recently during training, I posed the question to the room, "What are you trying to achieve on an inquiry call?"

We expected our salespeople would say their goal was to get a tour booked or something like that, and most of them did. Then we gave them each a pack of sticky notes. We told them to use as many sticky notes as they needed to write down as many things as they could that they were trying to achieve on an inquiry call. The lion's share of those goals were, as we thought, to get the tour.

They were all trying to get the customer to come into the building, which is important and not wrong, of course. However, it is an industry-wide type of inquiry. The ratio of people who are interested enough to call us and then who also move in is about ten percent. Inquiry to move-in about ten percent. This means that ninety percent of interested customers are lost, and in all likelihood this is because we didn't offer them the right next step. Somehow we lost the opportunity to continue the journey with those people.

For most people, when they call you, you are going to try to convince them that the tour is the best next step. But your job is to learn enough about them to create a compelling reason to tour. However, as you go through the process of learning enough about them, you may discover that the family is not prepared, whether it's emotionally, physically, or logistically, to come in for a tour.

In those cases, what other kinds of next steps do you have to offer? Interestingly, at this training a team member shared that one hundred percent of the time their job was to get that family into the building, no matter where they are in the buying cycle. This was a tricky moment for me. I had to say, "Well, not actually."

For those ten percent of people who are ready to find a place for their mom or dad to move into, the team member was absolutely correct. There are those ten percent who need to see it and experience it as soon as possible. But what about the other ninety percent?

Even in organizations with highly experienced salespeople, the usual sales strategy is to try to convince everyone to come in for the tour—"You're worried about your mom not taking her medications? Well, I'd really recommend you come in and talk to our nurse." But when everything is geared toward the closing ratio, it all becomes dependent on this one phone call. It all depends on you doing everything in your power to get them into the building. And the problem with this is that ninety percent of your customers will push back on coming in because they're not ready or they're in denial.

This is in contrast to what the Curiosity-Driven Sales approach is advocating. We urge you to learn more, whether or not the tour is the right next step for the customer. If you've taken the time to learn more, then when they do come in for the tour, you can really double down on providing them proof that your community offers what they need. You can tailor that tour to their specific situation and their specific needs because you learned so much about them.

Too often we haven't gotten enough information about the customer to learn where they are in the buying cycle so we can tailor the next steps to that, and as a result, too often they will feel rushed and decide to not come in at all.

The statistics tell the story. In my many years of analyzing sales metrics, I saw that 50 percent of the people who move in do so in the first thirty days after they've met you. The rest of the move-ins happen over a longer period, and these sales required patience. But here's an even more compelling statistic. Of all our leads, not just the qualified customers, but all the leads, only 10 percent will actually move in. What happened to the other 90 percent? In many cases, I suspect they felt rushed by a salesperson who was overly focused on filling a room and neglected to get to know the person and their situation well enough to know how to pace their sales process. In other words, they pushed too hard too soon.

Ninety percent. That's a lot of customers!

It's about meeting them where they are on their journey, understanding where they are, and tailoring your actions appropriately. If they are being discharged from the hospital and need to find a place in three days, you're likely not going to dig very deeply during discovery outside of understanding the care they require. You're going to get them into the community, match what they need to what your community can provide from a care perspective, and close the sale. But if you're treating everyone as if they're on that timeline, that literally pushes those potential customers into the 90 percent. Wouldn't it be nice to get a little piece of that pie?

When we're not nimble enough to adapt our strategy to

what they need, we are going to alienate them. We are only confirming for them that they don't want to do this. They are just looking for any reason to not do this, and you're giving them one.

Let's face it. If we are selling in a way that caters only to those people who have immediate needs because we are rewarded with the instant gratification of making our numbers right away, we are missing out on a lot of sales.

Consider for a moment if just 1 percent of the 90 percent of customers who either opted out or never heard back from you felt that you understood where they are in their decision-making process. If you are currently moving in six to eight people a month and most have an urgent situation, how does that impact resident length of stay? Let's not lose those sales, and let's find a way to add a steady flow of move-ins from people who had longer buying time frames.

Of course, we'll never get all of that 90 percent to move in, but it's still a very large pond. And we are only fishing with a small net. We're not casting our reel and then reeling and reeling and reeling them in a little bit more, slowly and carefully. We're just scooping some up with our net.

To use another sports analogy, if you're a sprinter and you're used to only sprinting, you're not going to be able to run a marathon as easily. But just remember that 90 percent of your leads are on a marathon course, whether they should be or not.

Keeping this in mind is very important for all salespeople, from experienced leaders to newbies. As a leader, if you're talking about how important it is to know your customers and then ending that sentence with what their closing ratio needs to be, you are talking out of both sides of your mouth. As a community-based salesperson, what you should be saying is "The more I know, the more I close." You should be saying, "I'm slowing down to go fast." And then you should actually do it. Stick to it, and don't waver. It works, and you'll help more seniors and make more money, spend less time on calls explaining why you're not having more tours and not achieving your budgeted move-in numbers, and be happier in your role. Win–Win!

That's where listening to learn comes in. Because of all the things you learned through listening and asking follow-up questions, you will offer advances and next steps that make sense with where the person is in the buying process. You will be able to create more compelling reasons for them to come in, because now you know enough that you can really build the value of coming in to see the community, whether they need to make a buying decision tomorrow or in a year.

It is all steeped in the knowledge that you acquire. If you only learn their dad had a fall, you'll have a difficult time differentiating your community with meaningful solutions that will enhance their dad's life. If your community is more expensive or maybe not as conveniently located as your competition, you've missed an opportunity to demonstrate the value of your holistic solution, and you've just lost that sale.

A QUICK WORD OF WARNING—DON'T LET CURIOSITY RUN AMUCK

When you learn something interesting about a customer and you want to learn even more about it, so you ask more questions and suddenly realize you've gotten off your sales path, you may be letting your curiosity run amuck. This is the opposite of telling a customer about your memory care neighborhood when they say that their mother seems confused. This is asking a question that is not aligned with your purpose. Keep in mind, you want to learn as much as you can about what they need so that you can tie it to what your community offers in a meaningful way.

As we established, this should not feel like the grand inquisition! You have to finesse your questions. There's a way to be curious that gets results and a way to be curious that does not get results. You have to pace the questions, and you have to pause and think sometimes, really reflecting in a purposeful way on what would be good for you to know so that you can help them. You need to also reflect back to them that you've just heard what they said.

You want to gather enough information that you can repeat the things they said back to them that warrant a next step. But if all you know is that their Mom has a UTI, that's going to be a very short summary. You haven't been curious enough, and you haven't listened to learn.

Offering a tour is never necessarily a wrong first-call objective. You just need to be armed with other things that may make more sense. And it will be much easier to have those other things if you've listened well and you know more because often it is premature to be focused on getting the tour.

The irony is that the tour is not going to be very effective if you make getting it your primary goal.

It's human nature that if you ask someone questions because you really want to better understand their situation and you really want to understand what that person is most worried about right now, it's going to feel like you care. If you just want them to come in for a tour, it does not feel that way. And if that second feeling represents what life will be like for their mom if she moves in, there will be a part of them that just doesn't feel great about it.

EVERYONE IS UNIQUE

You need to divorce your thinking from the other customers, because everyone is different and everyone has their own version of the common problems we see. Listening to learn helps us see what makes them who they are and what makes their situation unique.

We tend to batch people automatically, so it takes a shift in thinking to see everyone as unique. It's even more challenging because some people hide the ways in which they are unique. Sometimes your customers might not show their individuality very easily. People often have a protective mask on to try to not show their unique personalities, and it is difficult in any situation to be vulnerable with some stranger on the phone.

The customer is also making assumptions and batching you as a salesperson. They may be thinking, *I just want to know how much it costs. That's all I called for.* But we can't give them that because, of course, cost is so dependent on their particular situation and what level of care their mom or dad will need.

Your customer can spend seven minutes on a phone call with you, and during the call you just keep trying to tell them everything you have that they need, as opposed to spending those same seven minutes with someone who is really interested in their mom and what is going on with her. In that same seven minutes, the customer is going to feel more connected to the person that focused the conversation on what is going on with their mom and how it is impacting their life.

If you're really listening to learn, you're learning about their problems, but you're batching them by their problem. Once you find out what their problem is, there is another aspect to the technique, which is to see them as an individual, not just one of many people with the same problem. This is not the time to say things like, "I talk to families all the time that are in your exact situation. Here's what I recommend we do next." To demonstrate to them that you see them as an individual, you might say, "We often talk to families who have similar challenges with their mom or dad's health or with early stages of confusion, but I'd like to better understand what this looks like for your mom. Understanding that will make it easier for me to give you some good advice as to what might be the best thing for you to do next."

In the second case, you are bringing to light the fact that they are not alone but acknowledging that everyone's story is unique and their story has unique nuances. This helps you remember to stop thinking that everyone with the same situation takes the same next steps. You're saying they're not alone, and you're saying we have a solution, but you're not saying they are in the exact same situation as everybody else. At the end of the day, you're getting across a more caring message: You're not alone. We have a solution. But tell me what it looks like in your mom's life.

STAYING CENTERED

While all of this discovery is going on, and you are remembering all the things you want to do and say and all the things you don't want to do and say, you need to stay centered. Maybe you just got off the phone with a customer and walked out of your office, and maybe the maintenance director was supposed to move the model room for you because the family that is coming in soon wanted a high floor, so you need their model room to have a high floor. And the maintenance director starts telling you about all of the things he has to do, and therefore, he can't change the model room for you.

And then you turn to run to the bathroom, and you run into

the nurse who tells you she can't do the assessment that day on another family that was supposed to happen that day because she has to deliver all the medications and can't even call the family right now. She tells you that you need to call the family and let them know it's canceled for today and that they need to schedule another time for the assessment. You just wanted to go to the bathroom, and the model room is not going to get moved, and the nurse can't do the assessment. You go back to your office to start dealing with those two things, and the concierge calls and tells you you have an inquiry on line one. You may be laughing (or crying) reading this right now, but that is only because you've been there and you know it's true.

The question becomes how are you going to stay centered enough with all of that noise to really be present with this next family on the inquiry call? How do you take a moment to prepare and center yourself to do the best job you can to get these other important distractions off your mind?

You have to set all that noise aside for a little while. We use that exact example in our training to stress how important it is for you to give your best self and to really be able to listen when you pick up that phone. You need to take a beat. Sit down, try to relax, and count to twenty, which will probably only take you ten seconds, and then answer the inquiry call.

The important thing is to make sure that you are present for that person and that even though you may have heard a version of their story a thousand times, you haven't ever heard their story. The question really is, how do you bring yourself back into the mode of curiosity? How do you embody the person who has time to listen and be solely focused on this customer, not those two other things that hit you when you ran out of your office to go to the bathroom but instead only made it to the concierge desk?

Unfortunately, as we know, this whirlwind is our routine. Every day we are hit with these kinds of barrages of urgency, and usually it's exactly at the same time as we get an inquiry call or we have a family arrive for a visit. In these times, we have to take a minute, stop, and think to ourselves, *This is the first time I've heard this person's story.* You have to switch from a task-oriented mindset to a relationship-oriented one in a matter of seconds.

SELLING QUALITY OF LIFE

The customer doesn't call hoping you will care about them. Quite the opposite. They just want information. They just want to know how much it costs and whether you can help their mom deal with some memory loss. The magic happens, however, when you exceed that customer's expectations by demonstrating to them that this is not a commodity. This is not about how much it costs or even whether you help people with memory loss. What this is about is demonstrating what will matter to your mother's quality of life.

When we buy a car or a house, we innately understand what we are getting into. We know what we need to know in order to make this large purchase. Where is the house? How good are the schools? How old is it? How many seats does the car have? What's the gas mileage and the safety rating? But in our work, the vast majority of customers have no idea what they are getting into. You can begin to differentiate yourself right away just by how you respond to that inquiry call with an ability to understand what they are going through and listening to learn.

The point is to help them feel that people are going to answer their questions. They're not dropping a puppy off at the kennel for a weekend. You as a salesperson are delicately demonstrating the importance of gaining a deep understanding of their particular situation.

A caveat—there are some customers who really need to know how much it costs and are really not going to be willing to discuss anything else before they know that. That is all they want to know. They're thinking, *Don't ask me about what my challenges are right now, because I can't talk to you about anything until I know the price.* For those people, you definitely want to go ahead and give them some kind of ballpark price, usually a range depending upon the level of care, such as "It can run from $5,000 to $8,000 a month."

You need to understand what matters to your customer and what matters to their mom or dad. If you can set that tone early on in the process with a customer who is in that place in the buying process, then if you sense they need to know the price, give them the price, or you will lose the customer, because they don't care about any of the other things yet. This is not going to be a long call with someone who actually needs to talk to someone about all of what is happening with their mom or dad. They don't know how they feel about it. You have to be a student of people enough to recognize and understand all our different kinds of customers.

When you sense a customer can slow down and have a long talk, then absolutely that is what you should do—it will give them a sense of what this whole process of finding senior living should feel like. Trust me, your competitors are not going to help them feel seen and heard like that. They won't take the time; they're not slowing down to go fast and trying to know more so they can close more.

Your competitors are in more of an efficiency mindset. They've got an inquiry call, and they'd better get that tour scheduled. That mindset can drive bad behaviors. Not intentionally, of course, but it can end up being an uncaring approach. This uncaring approach doesn't help anyone. It doesn't help the customer feel seen and heard, it doesn't build trust, and it doesn't help you differentiate your community from the rest.

On the other hand, when you take every opportunity to listen and learn and form genuine connections with your customer, you have the ability to capitalize on what you've learned. And there is a world of difference between what those two things will feel like for the customer. Since our customers make their decisions based on how they feel, this will give you the edge.

If your inquiry call does lead to the customer scheduling a tour, then your efforts to listen to learn continue on the confirmation call you make before the tour. Now you have an opportunity to summarize again what you understand to be the things they are most concerned about and to let them know what you have lined up to show them or who you have lined up to come meet with them to address those issues. You can also make it a point to ask them whether, now that they've had a few days to think more about everything, there are any other concerns they have about their mom or dad that you can help them with on this visit.

On these calls, you are teeing up that customer to be thinking about their needs. You are reflecting back to them what they've already shared about their concerns. You can simply say, "Is there anything else we should make sure we have time for when you're here?"

ON THE TOUR

Listening to learn on the tour can take you to a whole new level of connection with the customer. At the start of the visit, it is one more opportunity to demonstrate that you hear them and you see them and their problems matter to you. You're saying, "As we talked about just the other day, I think it's really important for you to meet our nurse. She would like to talk to you about how she can help your dad manage his diabetes and insulin. Do we still have about an hour?" At every stage of communication, you're giving them the recap of last week's show, so to speak. You're reminding them of everything you've discussed so far.

As you continue to guide your customer on their buying journey, you are gathering implicit agreements as you go. You come to agreement on what is important to them, what they want to see in your community, and what their needs are. All the things that, if you're not aware of them, could become future objections. If you get all of those things out in the open, and you gain agreement with them all along while you're learning more about them, you will differentiate yourself, and that will continue throughout the entire life cycle of that sales process.

Methods such as these help you avoid solution selling, but they take work to learn. Following up with questions relative to a customer's answers is not as easy as it sounds. As you will see with this chapter's Get Curious exercise, this can be very tough to execute at times. You have to shut off the noise inside your mind that is only trying to close the sale and instead listen to the unique person in front of you with an open mind so that you can ask them another question based on their answer. Only then will you be able to dig deeper and find the treasure chest.

Often salespeople ask really good questions; the problem is the questions don't always pertain to the last answer the customer gave them, and they miss an opportunity to learn more. Part of the reason why this is difficult for salespeople is that you are supposed to prepare a set of questions in advance in order to be a good salesperson. That's what we are all taught. But those prepared questions can very easily lead you to stop listening, because you're thinking about how you're going to get your next question in. It's not like you are dismissing what they're saying as not important. It's just that you have already moved on in your mind to what you want to tell them or what you want to know next.

Just know that if you can do it, if you can follow the customer down the rabbit hole through answer-dependent questioning, it's a highly effective sales strategy.

As we've discussed, these are highly charged situations, and our customers are not window-shopping senior living. Your customers will also be learning, because they have a lot of questions and, again, they are highly emotional. They have deep concerns, and they often don't know what they don't know.

The back and forth between learning from being asked to think about things can be a great feedback loop. The questions we are asking the customer help them understand what kind of questions they should be thinking about. What are the nuances of this predicament, those issues they need to be thinking about as they move forward on their buying journey?

Sometimes as a salesperson you can be following along in the conversation, asking questions that relate to the last answer, and you may get to a point with a customer when it begins to feel uncomfortable. Perhaps you accidentally hit a hot button. Perhaps you are effectively asking the customer to be more vulnerable by answering the last question you asked, and they aren't comfortable with that much vulnerability. Particularly on the inquiry call, which is going to last only a few minutes, you probably won't get very deep. You should still be asking good questions, but you haven't earned the right yet to ask the hard questions because you haven't built the relationship yet.

Stay alert for signs that the customer's mood has shifted. It can just be a much longer pause on the other end that signals to you that you may have made the customer uncomfortable. Or the answer might suddenly be delivered to you in a different way, with a different tone of voice or a different type of vocabulary. You might be having a conversation with someone who gives you a lot of information at first, and then suddenly their responses switch to yes or no. These are all signs that you're trying to go somewhere emotionally they don't want to go. They might be just distracted by something going on in the room on their end, or it could be that you have taken the discussion to a degree of depth that they're not willing to go.

They may not be ready to talk about memory loss or a certain medical condition yet. They may only be realizing the severity of their situation for the first time on this call, in part because of your questions. If you don't listen, and you don't hear those signals or catch those clues that you need to slow down, you could inadvertently shut down the conversation, the learning, and ultimately the sale.

The same thing can happen in person, but it's far easier to notice. You can be in the middle of a fruitful discussion, and their body language can change from open to closed. It's difficult on the phone to employ techniques like mirroring because you can't see the person. On the phone, keen listening is vital in order to catch the audible cues. These are easier to mask than the visual cues. Either way, the message being sent by the customer is "Wait a minute, I think you've gone too far. I'm not comfortable with that, I don't like what I'm hearing, and I don't want to talk about it anymore." It's a shift in their energy, and even when you can't see them, you should be able to hear it if you are listening carefully.

Sometimes a family will come in for a tour with a difference of opinion among them over the search for senior living. There could be irritation among them, guilt, resentment, or a combination of all three.

It's common to have very difficult moments when a family is facing this reality or eventuality. This is where your empathy really needs to come into play. This is the time to adopt their perspective, put yourself inside their heads and hearts, and imagine what this must be like.

What can you do? You can acknowledge that everyone may be in different places and situations and express that it's really fortunate that the whole family is here. You can see they are all in different places and have different questions. You can say things like "Let me know if I'm on the right track. I think you're saying..." or "What I'm hearing is..." or "Are you saying that...?"

This ties into being your authentic self, which we will discuss in depth in a later chapter. But in this situation, just know that there will be differences of opinion and challenging moments. Your role at this point is to give them the space to express their individual concerns. You just need to be a real person and acknowledge them. You can say to a group who is clearly filled with different viewpoints, "We have a lot of decision-makers here today..." and focus on finding ways to equip all of those different decision-makers to go home and discuss this and figure it out, because you're not going to go there with them.

The most challenging tours are usually the ones when you

have the prospective resident and their husband, wife, daughter, or son. Often in assisted living, you are meeting with only the adult child, and more often than not it is the adult daughter. In these situations, you don't necessarily have to balance all the different perspectives of the family members. It's a little more of a controlled environment because you're dealing with someone who is in management mode.

But when you have the prospective resident there, it changes the dynamics. Because you want to make sure you are addressing and listening to the person who might be living there someday. You need to ask them questions, and depending upon where you are in the relationship with them, these could be very surface questions, such as "How are you feeling about this type of room? How important is the swimming pool to you? You've told me some of the things you need, but is there a way for some of these things that we've talked about to be managed for you at home?"

At the same time as you are talking to the prospective resident, you're talking to the adult child or other relative who is accompanying them and managing this. They have a lot of questions and needs as well. There might be dishonesty between the family members that is lurking beneath the surface, such as "He told me he quit smoking cigarettes, but my brother found an empty carton in the trash."

While it is more challenging to juggle the conversation between the prospective resident and their family on the tour, it's preferable to have both people there for a lot of reasons. The obvious reason is that seniors should have a say in what the next steps are for their living arrangements. Another reason is that with the prospective resident there, you're more likely to hear their objections, which will help you anticipate and prepare for any stumbling blocks along the way to a sale. The challenges arise when you're trying to balance a conversation between the person who might actually live there and their family member, both of whom might have very different—even opposing—concerns.

In the instance of our senior Edith, who isn't taking her medications regularly, she might say, "That's not true, I always take my medication. I eat a little something." Edith's pride is on the line, and it's human nature to put up a good front in these kinds of situations. But it can make it very tricky for you. Her daughter spoke to you at length about how she wasn't taking her medication because it upset her stomach, and it upset her stomach because she doesn't eat breakfast. You are aware that she is very worried about it. Now Edith is sitting in front of you, and you say something like, "I understand your stomach is getting a little bit upset when you take your medications and that you don't really love breakfast."

In this situation, you need to be careful with how you phrase things so that you don't accuse anyone of fibbing. You might ask more deeply about their medications. Try asking open-ended questions like, "Can you tell me a little bit about the medications that you're taking and how they make you feel?"

If they say, "Sometimes they upset my stomach," you might follow up with, "Oh, I'm sorry. How have you been trying to deal with that?" The goal is to give them a way to tell you the real story in a more natural way without judgment or stigma.

THEIR DENIAL AND YOUR EMPATHY

It helps to remember that for that prospective resident, there's often no problem they have to solve. They are likely to be in denial, but for whatever reason, they think they'll be fine living in their own home forever. Whether you are listening to learn or observing to learn, it comes down to understanding their experience and their perspective and having empathy for what is taking place and the impact it's having on everyone involved.

If you are simply coming from a place of wanting to better understand the situation, you'll do a better job of lowering their defenses. You want that prospective resident to be more and more open with you because you can't help them unless they really tell you about the problem.

Not only do they need to admit to the problem, you need them to tell you about it in as much detail as possible. It's impossible for you to provide a solution that makes sense to them unless you know a lot about the problem they need to solve. To do this, you need to make sure that your communication style with them is such that the relationship is growing and that you continue to see those defenses lowered.

You always want to be watching and listening. You might hear an objection that stalls the sales process somewhat, or they might just nod a lot, pretending they are going along with it when they are not. Whether it is verbal cues or body language, you want to make sure that those defenses are always coming down, not going up. Let's say one of your questions lands like a big lead balloon. How do you recover? How do you get back to a place where the defenses are lowered?

The best way is to come back to genuine curiosity. It's not about trying to be tricky, or deceptive, or manipulative, because you are engaging with them empathetically.

We need our customers to tell us the truth about what the biggest problem is, but we need to do this in a way that is authentic and genuine. If you're doing it just to achieve your goal, then it is a little manipulative. But we assert that you can use this strategy and still care. Strangely enough, that will give you a much higher likelihood that your efforts will pay off. And if you really do want to help, it shouldn't be that hard for you to care.

Key performance indicators matter. Efficiency matters. But your efforts to be efficient will be even more effective, and your metrics even more impressive, if you actually care. That is the irony. This is the heart and soul of going slow to go fast. This is about getting to the heart of the matter rather than dancing around the issues and wasting your time. If you build trust and develop good rapport with them, you will earn your way into the prospective resident or their family sharing with you the real challenges that they're having. It may feel like you're going slower, but you will close that sale much, much faster.

In my years of leading senior living salespeople, I have come to realize that there is a serious problem, and that is a lack of behaving with an empathetic nature. If you are not genuinely interested in understanding somebody's unique challenges, it will be very hard to demonstrate real empathy. And that sale is going to be a lot harder to close. If the family is not feeling authentic emotions coming from you, they are going to resist moving forward.

This is one of the most difficult and serious times in a person's life. So the next time someone tells you that their dad needs a salt-free diet, try to resist the urge to say right off the bat, "Our chef does that." Try instead to allow that information to open a door to an entirely new topic, such as the kinds of foods their dad can eat and enjoys eating. Every time you avoid solution selling, you are demonstrating that you are interested and that you care about the prospective resident's health and happiness.

If the salesperson had just asked Edith why she stopped eating breakfast, there would never have been an opportunity to learn that the medications were upsetting her stomach, because Edith would have just flat out denied it and the conversation would have stopped. Asking Edith to tell you a little more about what her typical morning looks like, however, has the ability to let loose a waterfall of information. Armed with that knowledge, you can figure out ways that your community can help a family solve one of their biggest problems.

Asking respectful questions that allow you to listen to the answers and learn will hinge on your ability to make purposeful word choices, which is the subject of our next chapter.

GET CURIOUS (IT TAKES PRACTICE)
THE ACTIVE LISTENING CIRCLE

In this exercise, the leader sits in the middle and represents the customer. All the people in the training represent the salesperson. You don't want more than five or six people in this exercise. As a group, the goal is to ask ten to twelve questions without offering a solution.

The first person has the easiest job, because nobody knows anything about the customer yet. Then, the next person has to ask a question based on the customer's answer. This continues around the circle, until everyone has gone twice. Everyone needs to follow the conversation as each answer is followed by a question relating to that answer. This forces people to listen and not get ahead of themselves.

HINT: Don't think about what question you're going to ask because it has to be based on the answer to the last question.

This is also helpful for learning to overcome objections. While you're in the circle, note anything you hear that might give you the opportunity to overcome an objection using the information coming in.

Chapter 5

Word Choice Matters

"Kind words can be short and easy to speak, but their echoes are truly endless."

—MOTHER TERESA

The words we use in senior living sales don't just convey information; they shape how people feel about the most difficult decisions in their lives. Using compassionate and clear language isn't just good sales practice—it's essential for building trust with families facing tough choices.

Let's say someone comes to you looking for memory care. Their mom has been wandering and was found most recently in her neighbors garage. You want to reassure them, and of course you want to sell them on life in your community, so you say something like, "You won't have to worry about that here, because we have a locked unit."

And then you wonder why they never schedule a tour.

The word locked is an institutionalized, punitive word—it's not a friendly, welcoming word.

A better approach would be to use words that are sensitive to the customers and the difficult situation they are facing. You could say, "Oh, yes, we have a memory care program located in our secured neighborhood" or "I understand. You must be worried about your mom wandering over to the nearby park. Our neighborhood is secured, and we have specialized programming for memory care."

These approaches offer a completely different representation of your community. "Locked unit" feels like they are institutionalizing the prospective resident, while "secure neighborhood" feels more like they're getting a big hug. One feels abrasive and, frankly, a little scary, while the other is comforting.

There are hundreds of examples of word choices in senior living sales that we can soften and humanize to help our customers feel more comfortable. For example, instead of "How is your mom's socialization?" try asking, "Does your mom visit with her friends much these days?" or "Tell me a little bit about how your mom spends her time with friends and family." With the latter question, you might learn that many of her friends have passed away, and her family is mostly busy living their own lives.

Think about it, nobody says socialization. Socialization is a word we associate with training puppies so they don't bite each other, or us. If you use that word with a customer, they might secretly wonder, *Will they treat me like a human being? Or a puppy?*

Most people think about these things in terms of being with friends, spending time with people we love, not socialization. Therefore, words like socialization are not words that

I advise you use with customers. But unfortunately, they're spoken every day in our profession. You may be thinking, *Not me, I would never say those words!* The truth is, these are things salespeople in our industry say all the time.

Remember that the words you choose offer your customer a preview of what life will be like in your community. They are hopefully going to move from a place where they're either living alone or living with their family (who've gotten a little tired of their stories) to an environment with people who are similar to them. They'll hear new stories, tell their own stories, and bond with people who have similar life experiences. They deserve to have these experiences and connections at this point in their lives. When they do make those connections, their son or daughter isn't going to say, "My mom is socializing a lot more." They'll say, "She's made a bunch of new friends! She hangs up before we're even done talking on the phone because she has to go play cards."

Another problem with these kinds of highly clinical questions is how easily they can turn into close-ended discussions:

"Are you worried about your mom's socialization?"

"Why yes, I am."

End of discussion.

Instead, you might try, "Tell me a little bit about what you think your mom might be missing since she's not able to spend as much time with her friends at the senior center anymore." Hopefully you can see that this is very different and likely to be much more effective.

EMPATHETIC WORD CHOICES

Being purposeful with your words and phrasing things that feel like natural, normal conversation can help your customers feel a little more comfortable about making this difficult choice. It is also essential to making people feel like they are unique individuals and that they matter. You can think of purposeful word choices as a way to express your empathy for their situation.

The healthcare industry comes up short on empathy too often. For instance, the doctors and nurses in hospitals are concerned about getting patients back to the baseline they were measured at when they first entered the hospital. But they don't stop to ask how this person was doing a week before they had the stroke or other emergency. The human being as an individual and their contributions to the world and their family tends to get lost in the systems their healthcare provider is moving them through. Senior living routines can fall into this as well. Sometimes we just seem to be going through the motions. And it's usually quite evident in the words we choose.

Word choice matters when it comes to how we refer to people as well. We might call an older gentleman who wanders sometimes a wanderer. He is not a wanderer; he's a human being who has lived a long life and happens to have some confusion now. We are only getting to see a tiny sliver of that long life, and we try to put him into a box called Wanderers. We batch him. It bears repeating that our job as senior living salespeople is to try to see the whole person so they can live their best life when they're moved in. Word choice is a powerful tool for doing just that.

Words have power. Words evoke emotion, and in my experience, emotion is one of the most powerful ways to move someone forward in a sale. There are words that pull your heartstrings, and there are words that close doors. It can be the exact same story, but if told in the wrong way, it can shut someone down. If told with thoughtful word choice, it can light someone up.

It is a painful experience for families to tour communities. It's not fun. People don't care whether you have a pizza oven or not. They care about their mom being well cared for. Often these families are about to do something they promised their parent they would never do. You need to be thoughtful about that. Your conversation with them is going to indicate how their parent is going to live the rest of their life, and this is the enormous responsibility you have in senior living sales. The responsibility is to listen to learn and be purposeful with your word choices.

If you are not thoughtful enough about the way you approach any given customer and the things you say to them, you are not going to necessarily get a second chance. Not only might they not choose to move into your building, they may choose to not move forward with senior living at all.

Everything you do and say is going to result in their making a decision one way or another. From the inquiry call through to your follow up, you want to be gently asking things like, "What's a typical day like for your dad? What does he like to eat for breakfast?" These kinds of questions are just more respectful, and they also allow you to listen and learn.

HEALTHCARE JARGON AND OTHER PET PEEVES

While senior living professionals may be used to terms like "ambulation" or "IL," this jargon may sound foreign and clinical to customers. By translating these terms into everyday language, you build rapport and understanding. I like to joke that salespeople in senior living could probably formulate an entire sentence of non-words using jargon. Ours is a very jargon-heavy world.

This chapter wouldn't be complete without my firm

reminder to resist using jargon. For instance, a customer calls and says, "I'd like to learn a little more about your community," and the director of sales asks, "Are you calling for IL, AL, or memory care?" The customer usually says something like, "Uh…I don't know. What's the difference?"

In senior living, one term we all use too much is ADL, as in, "How are your mom's ADL's?"

"I don't know. What is that?"

"Her Activities of Daily Living."

"Uh, I don't even know what that means."

"Oh, sorry. Is she making her own meals? Does she need any help in the shower?"

Sometimes I just want to ask, "Why didn't you just ask her *that*?"

Instead of being brave enough to ask that or something like, "Is your mom having any issues with her personal hygiene?" you blurt out, "Is your mom incontinent?" This kind of communication style is dehumanizing and can act like a verbal repellent for your customer.

Instead of saying "independent living," sometimes people get a little lazy, and instead of saying the whole words, they'll call it IL. No customer will know what you are talking about. They'll be confused. This is not the kind of conversation that evokes positive emotions or demonstrates the experience they'll have in your community, and it's certainly not the kind of talk that builds trust.

I hosted a coaching call just a few days ago where we focused on both word choices and listening. One of the salespeople on the call created the following inquiry questions: Is your mom ambulatory, and does she have any challenges with general mobility? How is her cognition? Are there ADLs you are specifically concerned about in her current situation? All of these things are important to understand, but they can widen the gap between the customer and you if they don't understand the clinical vocabulary. Using buzzwords like ambulatory and incontinence can whitewash the emotional pain of those realities with a coat of clinical vocabulary.

A better way to say it might be "Can you tell me about her daily routine? How is her memory loss impacting her life today? When it comes to getting ready for the day, does she struggle with anything specific? What worries would your mom have if you were planning an outing for the day?" These questions are phrased in a way the customer can clearly understand and answer, and they will likely get you the same information.

TALKING THROUGH SENSITIVE ISSUES

Choose your words carefully in situations such as these where you're discussing tricky subjects. For instance, you want to be mindful of how you talk with them about the loss of certain activities they used to enjoy. You need to learn more about the things they are no longer doing because sometimes, once they come to a senior living community, they can start doing those things again. These are often things you can talk about with them to help them see how your community will solve this problem for them. But how you phrase this matters, because you want to be sensitive to their feelings around this touchy subject.

Perhaps you're talking with a customer whose mom used to love to go to the senior center and play cards with her friends every week. Now, suddenly she's not interested in going anymore. What has changed for her mother? You could ask, "Is she having any issues holding the cards?" You may discover she has Parkinson's disease and that her mother has been self-conscious about her tremors and the ability to hold her cards. Also, if she was dropping cards and people were seeing her hand, she wouldn't be able to win as much, and people like to win.

The point is, once you gently find out about things they're not doing anymore that they used to love to do, try to discover the reasons for these changes. And the reasons behind those reasons as well. Tread lightly and kindly with your words, and you'll discover so much more.

PURPOSEFUL WORD CHOICES WORK

Being purposeful with your words is essential to helping people feel seen and heard. It's essential to treating people like the unique individuals they are, and it's essential for helping them feel like they matter. It is also absolutely essential to lowering their defenses and helping them become more open and vulnerable and thus willing to move forward on their journey toward selecting your community.

You will be a better salesperson if you do more of this. It will help you win more often. And at the same time, you will be helping a family feel comfortable enough to navigate a difficult transition.

Asking a customer about their concerns (in a respectful way) can also be an effective way to phrase your questions. For instance you might ask, "Are you worried that your mom's not spending enough quality time with her friends?" or "Are you worried that by her not going to the senior center as much, she's missing out on some of those rich relationships she's built with some of the ladies there?" That's very different from asking, "Are you worried your mom's not getting enough socialization?"

Nutrition is another buzzword to avoid. As a triathlete, nutrition is something I think of from a sports perspective. I need to know that I have quality calories going into my body to get me across the finish line. But nutrition is not a word I would say to my friends or even my coworkers. I would just say, "Hey, let's get some lunch. I feel like a salad."

But the reality is, many salespeople ask a prospective resident something like, "Can you tell me a little bit about your mom's nutrition?" These are clinical words and not generally used in day to day conversations outside of healthcare.

We need to be using normal, everyday language that comes to us naturally and sounds natural. If you're authentic, you're simply asking things like, "Has your mom been eating okay?" or "What does your mom usually have for breakfast?"

We don't use the word nutrition out in the normal world, so why do we use it so much in senior living? Especially when we are dealing directly with a customer, who has probably barely ever said that word before in their life?

Here are some other examples of questions using purposeful word choices:

- Are you worried that because...?
- How does your mom spend her time...?
- Tell me a little bit more about...
- Have you noticed any changes in...?
- How do you think your mom's feeling about...?
- Have you noticed any other times when...?
- What does a typical day look like for your dad?
- Are they having any issues with their personal hygiene?
- Are there certain things they're not doing as much anymore that they used to love to do?

By asking any of these types of questions, you are in some way getting closer to learning about things that are suddenly not happening anymore or things that have suddenly started happening that are concerning.

What's at stake is whether you are gaining their trust or not. What's at stake is making people feel seen and heard, because purposeful word choice means asking questions. It means having pure, deep curiosity. It's also about being a kind, caring person and having compassion for what your customer is going through. This type of approach opens up the window of opportunity for you to show them why your community offers all the things the senior in their life will need.

It comes back to the fact that you have an enormous responsibility. How well you demonstrate what your community offers will affect how this prospective resident will live the rest of their life. This will be their home—which is another opportunity to use purposeful word choices. You're not going to tell them that it will feel "like home." You're going to say that they will feel "at home." The difference is that one is an artificial replica, whereas the other is a real replacement.

TAKING A BREAK

In our earlier discussions of knowing when to get off the curiosity bus, word choice can help us navigate taking that break from discovery on a certain subject when it feels like the customer is on overload. We can say things like, "I'm sure this has been a very emotional conversation for you. I'm feeling emotional as well just listening to you tell me these things." You can pause at that point and maybe offer a recommendation as to what to do next.

Be sensitive to their state of mind. You wouldn't say, "What do you think we should do next?" because they are already overwhelmed and need time to process all the new information. You might try saying, "I think it might be a good idea right now for us to maybe just leave that thought for a minute. Why don't we talk about some of the other things that you wanted to talk about. We can come back to that after we let that sit."

At the end of the day, the issue that is overwhelming for them might be the biggest challenge they are facing. It might be the hundred-thousand-dollar issue, so it would be worthwhile for them to take some time and think it over, and worthwhile for you to allow them to do that.

In our work as salespeople, our goal is to lower the customers' defenses, which is better phrased "helping them feel comfortable," so that they will be able to make the best decision during one of the most difficult times of their lives. We need to continue to remember what a crucible moment this is for everyone, and we need to acknowledge the true crisis that our customers are experiencing.

Much of this boils down to you being your authentic self and putting yourself in the customer's shoes. If someone said to you, "Does your mom socialize much anymore?" how would you feel? If they said, "Does your mom get to spend much time with her friends these days?" how does that feel? If it was your mom, how would you feel? If you were asking your good friend about their mom, how do you think they would feel?

Our work is difficult enough already. We don't need to use words that we think will convey our expertise and professionalism like nutrition and socialization. They don't come off as warm. Just talk to your customers about what the next steps might be for their mom or dad who has fallen a few times or whose neighbor keeps calling you because their parent has locked themselves out of their house accidentally again. These are situations where you might say, "That must be really scary" or "That sounds frustrating."

To connect with your customer, you can simply be your authentic self. Work on forming a genuine connection. If you're the kind of person who asks people if they socialize, then go ahead and use that term. If you're the kind of person who wonders what kind of nutrition they should order off the menu, then by all means, say that. I understand that sometimes it makes us feel more credible to use that kind of vocabulary. But in fact, we are at our most credible, our highest performance level, when we speak in ways that help others feel comfortable.

When you think about word choices from a sales perspective, it's simply to talk in a way that the customer will understand. Don't make people who are having a hard enough time making a tough decision try to decipher what ADL means. Just ask, "What are some of the things she does everyday?" or "What does her everyday life look like?"

Of course, you need to be able to learn things that will advance the sale. "How much help will she need getting ready for the day? What medications is she taking? Does she have any difficulties making her meals?" At a certain point, you need to know these kinds of things. You don't need to know them right away. But when you do need to know them, you can simply ask, "Does your mom have any trouble getting ready for the day?"

The serious piece of all of this that falls on you, the salesperson, is that the preparation for everything you do and everything you say is key. It has to be purposeful. The responsibility you bear as a sales professional is to learn as much as you can by asking great questions, which will help you and your customer understand whether senior living at your community is the right next step. This takes planning on your part to ensure you get to the heart of the matter.

WORD CHOICES WITH YOUR TEAM

In my work as a leader in sales, I've become very mindful of my word choices. When I was at Sunrise Senior Living as the SVP of sales, I learned over the many years how leveraging language can clear the way for people to share their challenges openly and honestly. It also allowed me to take a situation where someone may need to improve a specific skill and have a conversation about how they can do "even better" versus "not good enough." As leaders we should never leave people feeling like less. Instead, our role is to find the trigger that inspires people to work a little harder, be more comfortable with being uncomfortable, and understand that what they need to accomplish is possible.

We also need to show support for all team members, not just some of them. We created a fund that employees could donate to through payroll deduction. The fund was for team members who had catastrophic hardships and through applications could be awarded financial assistance. At annual conferences we would rally team members to participate by signing up for payroll deductions as a way to ensure the fund could help as many people as possible.

Our approach to make this happen was to ask everyone to think about a care manager who always shows up for work, is always a pleasure to be around, and works really hard. We asked them to keep that person in mind when they thought about this fund. We said something like, "Imagine if that person had a financial hardship, something that could not only prevent them from working but also create some radical life change for them."

We found it effective because rather than using guilt or pressure tactics to persuade people to donate, we were able to inspire them to do a good deed knowing they now had a different perspective on who the fund supported. The word choices made all the difference, and this is an influential sales tactic no matter what you are trying to achieve.

One way to approach this is to ask yourself whether your words are going to convince someone to work harder or merely make them feel bad.

I learned early on as I started becoming responsible for other salespeople and conveying messaging to large crowds that gaining buy-in from your listeners, getting people to step up, requires that you treat them with care and respect. They will work harder if you say, "We could do even more" or "We could be even better" than if you tell them their occupancy rate is terrible.

How are you going to get your message across to your salespeople in a way that makes them feel like they can do what you're asking them to do instead of making them feel like they aren't good enough?

Try asking yourself which words will create barriers to connection and which words will encourage connection. Which words will inspire people to do things that make them uncomfortable or that they just don't like doing even though it is a critical part of their job.

Too often, in my opinion, leaders leverage fear and shame in an attempt to improve performance. It doesn't. Being on a call or in a meeting where you are told, "You don't have enough leads. You need to do more business development. You must be doing something wrong because you are not getting enough second visits" is not helpful. I bet, for example, in regard to business development, they already knew the business development fell short, because that happened when they didn't do any business development.

As a leader, your job is to ensure they have what they need to be successful and assist in problem-solving. As I shared earlier, people will tell you their challenges if they trust you and your intentions. If they don't, it's hard to understand the actual problem enough to find a solution. So instead of saying, "You are not doing the required number of business development appointments" try, "it looks like something got in the way last week that kept you from getting your business development done, how can I help?" This assumption of a barrier vs. a "you just didn't do it" can lead to an open dialogue about the real issue. Then you can actually help.

Over time, as I continued to work on this myself in my roles as a leader, I became passionate about how important purposeful word choice is in everything we do in sales.

Word choice also applies to all of the other principles in this book. It helps people feel seen and heard, it allows you to slow down and listen to learn, it gives customers a preview of what life is like in your community, and it most certainly builds trust.

Just be human. It's the most effective way, because it helps your customers feel comfortable. Helping your customers feel comfortable is an effective sales tactic in many ways, and one of the most subtle yet powerful ways is that it builds trust during this very serious period in someone's life. In the next chapter, let's take a look at how building trust in the discovery process often stems from curiosity-driven, authentic interactions with your customers.

GET CURIOUS (IT TAKES PRACTICE)
MUSICAL JARGON CIRCLE

This is a dynamic and engaging exercise designed to help sales-people eliminate jargon from their language and focus on plain, empathetic communication.

Instructions:

1. **Form a Circle:**
    - Gather about six participants in a circle. The training leader will stand in the middle, playing the role of the "customer."
2. **Scenario Setup:**
    - The training leader provides a basic profile of the customer, including their needs, concerns, and relevant details as if this were an inquiry call for senior living.
3. **The Game Begins:**
    - Each participant takes turns asking questions to the "customer" (the training leader) in a way that helps them understand the customer's needs and gather vital information.
    - The challenge is to avoid using any industry jargon, acronyms, or overly clinical terms like "ADLs" (activities of daily living) or "nutrition."
    - If someone slips and uses jargon or a technical term, the training leader taps them on the shoulder, and they must step out of the circle.
4. **The Circle Shrinks:**
    - As in the game of musical chairs, the circle keeps getting smaller as participants are eliminated for using jargon.
    - Eventually, only one or two salespeople are left stand-

ing—those who have successfully avoided jargon and asked clear, meaningful questions.

5. **Debriefing:**
   ○ Once the winners are declared, the group should debrief together.
   ○ Discuss how it felt to avoid jargon and how some salespeople found creative ways to express ideas in simple, customer-friendly terms.
   ○ Reflect on how avoiding technical language helps build rapport and foster understanding with the customer.

Purpose of the Exercise:

- This activity reinforces active listening and empathetic communication while encouraging salespeople to find accessible ways to describe their community's offerings. It's a fun and practical way to build better sales habits while also showing how easy it can be to rely on jargon—and why avoiding it matters in senior living sales.

This exercise tends to be both entertaining and insightful, giving participants a deeper understanding of the power of words in shaping customer experiences.

Chapter 6

Finding Opportunities to Build Trust

"Trust is the glue of life. It's the most essential ingredient in effective communication. It's the foundational principle that holds all relationships."

—STEPHEN R. COVEY

When my father's wife was close to the end of her life, he needed my help finding senior living, and I accompanied him to a few assisted living communities. His wife's daughter and my three siblings had other obligations and did not come along; however, we knew they would of course be involved in the decision-making process down the road. Everything my dad and I did would have to be conveyed to them so they could participate in the discussion and the choice, and it fell to me in particular to relay our findings to all of them and explain why my dad and I felt good about a particular place.

I was not alone in this. For most families, when they begin the uncomfortable process of searching for senior living, there is usually one token child who is doing the legwork. This is usually the sibling who lives nearest to the parent, the one who has the most time, or both. While there are many facets to building trust in senior living sales customer relations, one of the most important ways we can build trust is to help that one sibling maximize their capability to communicate your brand promise to the rest of the family.

Having been on the other side of a complicated sales process such as this, I know how vital it is for the salesperson to equip one sibling who has been put in charge to share what they have learned and why some things matter more than others in making such an important decision.

In a sense, you, as the salesperson, become the influencer to the whole family. Everything you get across to the customer has to also influence all these other people who you most likely will never even meet. And while every family is different and unique, many of the dynamics are the same. A family, often with conflicting values, needs, and wishes, all has to work together to make this extremely expensive and difficult decision. Often, they don't live close to each other. Often, they can't all find the time to visit the communities.

YOUR ROLE AS CONDUIT TO THE FAMILY

In these situations, your job becomes to equip that one family member who will be the spokesperson for the family, the one who is your primary contact, with information that will help them explain all of the nuances of what your community offers to the rest of the family clearly and, of course, in a positive light. This is where you can do all of the great things we've discussed so far—in short, build a rapport with them and build a genuine relationship. When the time comes, you can ask them, "How ready do you feel to talk about this with the rest of the family?"

They may say, "Well, I don't feel ready at all."

In this case, you can ask if there is anything in regard to the programming that you've spoken with them about that they'd like to discuss more. "As we're getting closer to you and your father deciding, what I'm hearing is that some of the most important things for your dad's wife are to have a room on the first floor and to make sure that we can put a bird feeder outside of her window so she can see the birds when she's lying in bed. Also, that the food she'll be getting is food she likes and that she'll be taking her medications on time. Is that about right?"

You might also ask them, "So, as you're preparing to go back and chat with Tony and Lisa"—calling their siblings by name because you know their names by now, because you listened to learn—"is there anything you don't feel totally comfortable talking about during the family meeting tomorrow night? Anything else I can help explain or discuss with you more?"

At this point, because you haven't done an assessment yet and you may not be able to give them an exact cost, they might say, "Well, I'm still not clear enough about the cost."

Unfortunately, you may be in a situation where you can't give them a hard dollar amount, because it depends on their needs in terms of level of care. You might say, "Okay, that's fair. I know that might feel really frustrating..." and recommend you go ahead and get that assessment. Again, you are talking to your customer like you would talk to a friend. You're not trying to steer the conversation to a place where you're more comfortable. You're staying in a place where you're willing to be the conduit to their family, whether you're making the sale or not.

You should be able to say things like, "I know this will be a difficult conversation with them. It's hard even under the best of circumstances. So please let me know what else you need to know or understand so that I can help you all make a great decision."

In this scenario, you are being as transparent as possible, and you are being mindful that this is not your only customer. There are many other family members involved behind the scenes. You are also demonstrating how the prospective resident will feel if they move in by showing them that you care about helping them with this difficult conversation and decision.

Everything we've discussed in the previous chapters is about building trust. Recognizing the high risk and high emotion of the situations our customers are in, helping them feel seen and heard, listening to learn from them, applying curiosity in our sales tactics, and choosing our words purposefully are all ways we can build trust with our customers in order to form genuine connections with them that help them feel more comfortable and choose our community.

We are in the business of building trust, because if our customers don't trust us, they won't tell us the truth. They won't share their whole story, and if we don't hear the whole story, it will be very difficult for us to tie our solution to their greatest need.

NO BROKEN PROMISES

Number one on the list of trust-building behaviors is to keep your promises. This is a no-brainer. Just do what you say you will do. If the customer thinks you're going to call them on Tuesday because you told them you would, then call them on

Tuesday. When you make a promise, do so with the intent to keep it.

Senior living is a people industry, and things go wrong every day. Parents and adult children get upset every day. You are going to be dealing with difficult situations every day. And families will continue to deal with more difficult situations once they move in. Sometimes the family will give you the benefit of the doubt if you slip up on a promise or neglect to show them something they've expressed as a concern. But if you want to win more often, you'll aspire to get to the place where you are building trust and they don't have to give you the benefit of the doubt.

Everything you do, positive or negative, demonstrates what it will be like if they move in, and aligning your actions with your brand promise is another way to build trust. If you don't, you'll lose the sale, because the family will feel the lack of alignment and decide to do something altogether different. The importance of building trust cannot be understated.

If you don't build trust, it can elongate the sales process. But when you do build trust, you can significantly shorten the sales process by doing something so different from your competitor, so demonstrative of your brand promise, that they want nothing less for their loved one.

Building trust starts with returning their very first phone call as quickly as you possibly can. That responsiveness signals your reliability and caring from the very start. It puts an exclamation point on showing them they matter.

Keeping your questions open-ended also builds trust. It displays your curiosity and thus builds trust because it shows that you're interested. Asking the kinds of questions we discussed in chapter three helps them feel like when their loved one moves in here, people will really care about them, be interested in them, and take time for them.

If all you're asking is "what's wrong with you right now" kind of questions, not only will you sound like every other salesperson they have talked with, but these questions limit the amount of insight you can learn about the prospective resident. "How many medications are you taking?" A lot, so what? When a salesperson takes the time to have a genuine conversation with their customer and doesn't just want to know what their budget is or how quickly their mom will be discharged from the hospital, it makes a difference.

These are people seeking help at a very difficult time, searching for a solution to a problem they may not fully understand. They're not looking for tasks or checklists. They're human beings and they may not be consciously processing their reaction from being dehumanized by those questions, but they will get a feeling in their gut that the interactions with their salesperson don't feel quite right.

SUBTLE MANIPULATIONS AND SOLUTION SELLING

If you were the prospective resident and you said to me, "I'm having trouble with making sure I'm taking my medications on time" or "I'm not eating a lot of my meals like I should because I'm feeling full more quickly, and I just don't have that kind of hunger," it could be an appropriate time to tell them about your chef's delicious home-cooked food, but that would be leaning toward solution selling.

If you think about it, a better question to ask them is whether feeling full more quickly has impacted their ability to take their medications at all. This way you are layering those deeper discovery questions into a natural conversation, and you end up with important information enabling you to help them. All of this builds trust because not only are you learning things, you're learning through genuine conversation, not just a routine interview where you are just trying to check all the boxes.

There are examples of subtle manipulation through information-seeking by salespeople all the time in our daily lives. When you go on the Internet and want to learn about something, such as a vacation in the Canary Islands, you type in your search terms and find a website that seems to be filled with useful information. However, if they won't give you any information until you give them your email address, how do you feel? I personally feel like I'm being held hostage for information. I have to clear all of these hurdles in order for me to learn more about what I'm interested in. It doesn't feel good.

Every senior living company has things that they can and cannot provide. No one has everything. And you have to communicate many of those things, but not right at the top of the call. I appreciate that as salespeople, your time needs to be revenue generating. But if you shoot that information at them right away, you will alienate them, as opposed to asking curiosity-driven questions that will bring out the other information and in a more natural way.

If you say for instance, "You shared that you've lost a lot of weight recently. Tell me a little bit about how you're eating."

They might say, "Well, I don't really like the stuff that people bring me."

So you say, "So it sounds like someone is bringing you food?"

And then you learn that they're using Meals on Wheels, and it sounds like they don't like the food they're getting from it.

"No, I don't."

"Well, is there anything you're eating instead of those meals?"

"No, I don't cook anymore."

Through this interchange, you have learned so much, and without alienating them through an onslaught of checkbox questions and without having to ask them, "Are you able to make your own food?"

Instead, you are using purposeful word choice to ask purposeful questions. Everything is connected, and really the connective tissue here is building trust. Your body language and word choice most definitely come into play when building trust.

You will either open people up and make them feel like you are worthy of their trust, or you will shut them down and help them feel like you are not worthy of that trust. Word choice matters dramatically in terms of trust building outcomes. And so does the tour.

TRUST ON THE TOUR

Let's say I ask a salesperson what they plan on showing a particular family when they come in for a tour.

The salesperson says, "Oh, I'm going to give them the standard tour."

My reaction to that is going to be "There's no such thing as a standard tour. By this point you should have gathered enough intel to personalize their tour."

The salesperson vaguely remembers that the daughter said her mom was a big reader, and they told her about their large and inviting library. But they also remembered that the customer told them on the phone that their mom had been found wandering recently and seemed more confused in general. When they come in, instead of building trust by taking them first to the library, the salesperson isn't thinking about the library and is only focused on taking them to memory care. She takes them to that neighborhood and shows them how secure it is and describes the programming. They barely have time to peek into the library after that.

The problem with this is that even though the family definitely should see and learn more about the community's memory care offerings, what was at the top of the customer's mind was the library. This is about meeting them in the moment.

In this moment, they want to know their Mom's love of reading will be fostered and supported if she moves in here. Paying close attention to what they say they're interested in or concerned about rather than what you think they should be interested in or concerned about sends the message that you see and hear them and that you respect their wishes. This can build a lot of trust.

What's important to understand is that we learn some of their story over the phone through discovery discussions and in person when they first arrive. If you are very upfront with the customer and ask, "If you leave with nothing else today as you're beginning to gather your information, which two things are you the most interested in seeing?"

If they say, "The library and the dining hall," then even though you know their mom will need memory care, then please, show them the library and the dining hall. Just try to be in this moment with them.

This isn't about you forcing them to be on your sales process timeline. You are on their sales process timeline, and at this point, they may not be able to retain all of the information. Maybe they should be more worried about something other than the library, but they're not. What you as the sales professional think they should be worried about is not the issue.

You have to give credence to them in this moment. This is what they think is important. So that's what we are focusing on. Listening to their concerns and addressing those concerns at this time is what they will remember. If you do it this way, they will tour five different communities and see all the things everyone always has, but since only you tailored the tour experience for them by taking them to the library first, you will stand out as the most trustworthy.

It may help to keep in mind that this isn't the only chance you have to show them everything. You can say something at the end of their tour such as "I know some of the things you might want to see we didn't get to today. Are those things you feel you really would like to see today, or do you feel like you're getting to a position where you've got enough information right now to share with your family?"

Most everyone on the tour will get to see a model room and the dining and activity rooms. But only some people make it clear they're interested in something that is specific to their lifestyle—the library, the garden area, the beauty shop—those kinds of things. Listen to learn and then show them what they've said they want to see! This will go a long way toward building trust.

If there are some important elements that they should be seeing, such as memory care, then maybe you should have asked better questions that would help them realize it would be important to see that on the tour. If you had gotten them to say something like, "Well, since the neighbors have found her outside their house three times in the last month, we should probably see the studio apartment in memory care," that would be doing your job as the salesperson, stirring the conversations up enough to bring out the vital needs so that you can understand everything they should see.

TRUST AFTER THE TOUR

Building trust through personalizing their experience also takes place beyond the tour. It is their entire journey with you as they make their senior living decision.

I remember a woman from a long time ago whose salesperson found an opportunity to build trust through follow-up efforts. She grew orchids, the most finicky of all flowers. In the follow-up note the salesperson sent, she included a little pamphlet she had found on orchids. In the note she wrote, "After hearing you talk about orchids, I became curious and wanted to learn more. I found this little book and thought you might like it too." These kinds of small but big actions take it to the next level in your efforts to build trust.

Personalization and helping someone see that they will be able to feel at home in your community are not easy. In the next chapter, we will dive even more deeply into giving your customers a preview of what life will be like in your community by getting creative about what you do with all of the information you have acquired through your Curiosity-Driven Sales strategies.

If you take one thing away from this chapter, let it be this: taking every opportunity to build trust is one of the most effective ways for you to close more sales.

GET CURIOUS (IT TAKES PRACTICE)
THE TAILORED EXPERIENCE WORKSHEET:
BUILDING A PERSONALIZED STRATEGY
Purpose:

This worksheet is designed to help you reflect on your interactions with prospective residents and their families, ensuring that your next steps are aligned with what you've learned through active listening and to identify what more you need to know. By systematically evaluating what you know, challenging assumptions, and building a tailored strategy, you can move the customer closer to making a decision.

Worksheet Instructions:

1. **List everything you know about the prospective resident and their family.** Begin by writing down all the facts you've gathered about the resident and their family's needs, preferences, interests, and concerns. Be as specific as possible.

2. **Challenge the facts to ensure they are not assumptions.** Review the list carefully. Ask yourself whether these are things you actually know or if they are assumptions you've made based on limited information.

3. **Acknowledge what you need to learn more about.** Identify gaps in your knowledge. Are there areas you haven't explored yet? What additional questions can you ask to fill in the blanks?

4. **Validate or disprove any assumptions.** If you've realized that certain points are assumptions, make it a priority to confirm or disprove them through further conversations with the prospect or their family.

5. **Dig deeper into their needs and preferences.** Are there unspoken needs or preferences that you haven't yet uncovered? Use your curiosity to guide deeper questions about their interests, concerns, or dreams for the future.

6. **Build a list of follow-up activities you've done thus far.** Write down the actions you've taken since your last interaction with the prospect (e.g., follow-up emails, phone calls, sending information, etc.).

7. **Consider how closely your follow-up matches what the**

customer needs. Evaluate how well your follow-up activities have been tailored to the specific needs of the prospect. Did your follow-up resonate with them or feel generic?

8. **How tailored has your follow-up been thus far?** Be honest: did your follow-up reflect what you learned about the resident's personal needs and preferences, or was it more focused on general selling points?

9. **Did your follow-up validate "I hear you, I see you, and you matter"?** Review whether your interactions have made the prospect feel heard, seen, and valued. Reflect on whether you've acknowledged their concerns and interests in a meaningful way.

10. **Decide on the next steps to move the prospective resident and their family forward.** Based on what you now know, outline the next best steps for follow-up. Whether it's providing additional information, addressing new concerns, or offering another tour, make sure it's tailored to their situation.

By consistently going through this process, you'll be able to identify opportunities to build trust throughout the sales process by offering tailored next steps and recommendations aligned with where the customer is in their decision-making process.

Chapter 7

Giving a Preview of What Life Will be Like

"If you can't do great things, do small things in a great way."

—NAPOLEON HILL

If you go to a hotel and the people at the front desk don't seem very attentive when you're trying to check in, and then you get to your room and there is dust on the coffee table or the bedspread isn't made the way it's supposed to be, and then you go to the restroom and it just looks a little grimy, how do you feel? You don't feel good about it. And you think to yourself, *Everything here is grimy*. You don't think to yourself, *The desk clerk and the bedspread and the coffee table were a little disappointing*. You think, *Everything is grimy here*.

If this particular hotel was a Marriott, you might even think to yourself, *This doesn't feel like a Marriott*. Marriott, of course, has a brand image that you've come to rely on. Things are clean, people are friendly, and the housekeeping services are reliable. There is a sense that you're supposed to know what you're getting. But then if you get there and the desk person is too busy talking with their co-workers to help you, you feel like something isn't right.

Similarly, if you are visiting a community and the forks they put down on the table look like they maybe didn't go all the way through the dishwasher, you think to yourself, *I'm not sure I want my mother to eat here.*

These are all little things. But in many cases, it's the littlest things that make the biggest difference.

Little things all add up. Too many little things go wrong, and it doesn't feel great. When it doesn't feel great, they start thinking things like, *They can't even wash their forks properly, so I'm never going back.*

It's little things like the senior living community concierge who is juggling vendor and family arrivals, on top of residents waiting for the community bus to go to an event, all while the phone is ringing. She is not very friendly when she answers that phone, and the customer feels like they're bothering her. Maybe she uses jargon they don't understand, such as "Are you looking for AL or IL?"

That's when they say, "I'm sorry, what's AL? I'm looking for a place for my mom." But they're thinking, *We're definitely not moving our Mom in here.*

NO ONE WILL BE DANCING

If you think about it, people are either going to feel a little bit better after coming to see your community or they're not going to feel a little better. Either way, your customers are not going to start dancing around the room filled with joy no matter what you do. Shopping for senior living is not fun for anyone, ever. But it has to be done, and you have the opportunity to make your customers feel just a little better. If you do, you will stand out, and you will more likely get the sale over your competitor.

When we acknowledge what an enormous responsibility you are taking on, we realize we need to treat this person accordingly. Everything we do and say will be magnified. If a customer sees what looks like a dirty fork, they will think, *They don't wash the dishes very well here.* If the customer stands at the concierge desk while waiting for someone to acknowledge them, the customer will think, *They don't seem very attentive here. I wonder if my mom would have to wait a long time when she needs help.* You get the point. Everything people see, hear, smell, taste, and touch is translated in the customer's mind into *This is what life is like here in this community.* It may or may not be subconscious, but either way it will leave an unsettling feeling.

This is when we must keep every single one of our promises. From a sales perspective, when we're not prepared with a well-designed, tailored tour for the customer, and we don't keep our promises, the customer doesn't feel any better and we don't get the move-in.

If we agreed that we were going to talk on Tuesday at two o'clock but you got busy, so you pushed that phone call to the next day, you're not keeping your promise. As you go through your post-call review, you realized you decided for a reason that it would be a good idea to call on Tuesday. You had a reason for that. So now, not only have you broken your promise to your customer, you've broken your promise to yourself.

All of the great things you're sharing with the customer sounds good to them, but then you drop the ball. They told you they were talking to their sister on Wednesday, and they had talked to you a lot about their mom's Parkinson's. You said you found a really great article on Parkinson's, and you were going to send it to them before Wednesday so they could use that and share it with their sister when they talked, but the email with the article never came because you forgot to send it. They realize that you don't do what you say you're going to do, and that little thing—the article—becomes a big thing: the sale.

That customer was counting on you to help her convince her sister. But you didn't send the article, so now the customer is not as prepared to talk to her sister. Unfortunately for all of you, the sister might be the biggest obstacle to getting their mom to move in.

This connects to the customer not feeling like you see and hear them. If you told them you were sending them an article, sending it signals that you actually care, and it sets the foundation for them to feel that you will keep your promises.

Maybe a customer tours a community at three o'clock in the afternoon, and the dining room chairs are all out, and the remains of lunch are still on the floor because it has not been vacuumed. The customer glances in and thinks, *They can't even vacuum the floor. How can we expect them to care for our mom?*

THE LITTLEST THINGS

I have come to realize how important the little things are. You have to get many, many little things right in order for someone to make this decision in your community's favor. We are talking about how they will take care of someone they love most in the world. But they only wash their forks some of the time. *Maybe today Mom will get a clean fork, maybe she won't? Hmm. I don't think so.*

That is what they will be thinking.

The tour is probably the most impactful way to build trust with your customer. Because this is when it becomes real to them that they will be trusting you to take care of this most important person at the most vulnerable point in their life. And the community down the street costs a thousand dollars a month less than yours does.

You're not just cheating yourself out of a sale if you let your customers down or don't show them everything they should see when they come on the tour. You're doing the customer a grave injustice because you're depriving them of the chance to experience the lifestyle and quality care that you provide.

If we accept the premise that very likely this is the first time someone is having to make a decision like this for somebody else, we need to realize that people's understanding of what senior care is, is often very different from the reality. If you ask most people about senior care, they picture a very sad place.

Usually, the customer is going to spend between forty-five minutes to two hours on that in-person tour. So you have as little as forty-five minutes to help them walk away with an understanding of what life would be like for someone if they chose your community.

One salesperson I know had a prospective resident who was coming in for an event and had learned the following day was her one hundredth birthday. The salesperson filled out a large, oversized birthday card with notes sending birthday wishes. She also reached out to the prospective resident's daughter and asked for some gift ideas and learned that her mom loves pansies. She shared that her mom always had the front porch planter filled with pansies, so at the event, they gifted her the card and the pansies. How must that had made her and her daughter feel? Seen and heard? Yes. As you may have assumed, this story had a happy ending as she loved everything, and soon afterward, she moved in. She also runs the garden committee, and you can bet their front porch always has pansies. It's the little things.

You only have this one finite moment in time to help someone understand what life will be like in your community. They have no idea what they should expect. Sometimes they don't even know what a good senior living community should feel like or look like. Because of this, you have an opportunity to show them what a good one should be like. You can do this by giving them a highly tailored experience that reflects what you've learned about them through curiosity and listening to learn, all of which takes planning.

IT DOESN'T HAPPEN BY ACCIDENT

If you really want to represent what life will be like if they move in, you have to accept that it can't happen without a plan. Often prospective residents only meet the salesperson prior to making the move-in decision. Even on the tour, prospective residents and their families only engage with the salesperson. When you have created a compelling reason for a tour of the community, you have an opportunity to further demonstrate what it will be like to live there. If she moves into the community, she will interact with many team members and other residents; this is a chance to show those people off and give a real sense of your community. A great tour experience includes key team members, especially the executive director.

Planning doesn't stop there. You need to consider what will be most important for the prospective resident and their family to see and experience. Generally speaking, they don't need to see the entire community or learn about all of the wonderful programs you offer. Showing them what is most important to them (which you learned through discovery) will demonstrate you listened and learned. Now, after you confirm with the customer what is most important to them, let them know what they will be seeing and experiencing. And then ask, "Are there any other parts of the community you would like to see while you are here today?"

When you consider what the customer is "buying," it goes way beyond care and a suite. You are selling them a lifestyle, new friends, new things to learn through your programming, and people who will love and care for them. I've often said that the salesperson's role in selling senior living is helping a family understand that senior living could be the right solution and that a tour is the right next step. Everyone else—the team members and the residents—actually closed the sale. Since they're your closers, they need to be involved from the very beginning.

After they move in, you won't really be in the prospective residents' lives anymore. They might see you in the hallway once in a while, but they don't have any reason to interact with you anymore. And your job at that point is to go out and find another customer anyway. But if you've listened to and learned in preparation for this customer's tour, and you understand their high priority needs and concerns, you create an experience that will give them what they need, and they will walk away knowing what life will be like if their loved one moves in.

If we go back to the dining room with Angela's mother, Louise, who won't take her medications because she's not eating well and the meds are upsetting her stomach, then on her tour, what should be communicated loud and clear to her are that the care manager in charge of medications and the dining service coordinator are going to meet with her when she comes. These people are going to learn all about her mom's situation and be on board to help. Once she knows this, Angela will feel relieved. She will feel like someone else besides her cares that her mother isn't taking her medications.

You want your customers to have an opportunity to not just shake hands with the care coordinator and the dining services coordinator. You want to schedule a period of time when those team members can sit with your customer and demonstrate to them what they can expect from your community—a caring team who will problem-solve with Louise to ensure she is enjoying her meals and taking her medications.

When your customers have an experience that is personalized and they are given an opportunity to talk with the people who will be there for the prospective resident if and when they move in, that is a differentiator. It will leave an impression and greatly affect the customer's decision-making process.

Think about it—all of the senior living communities Louise and Angela are touring have someone to lead care, someone to assist with medications, and someone who cooks. But because you've listened to learn, and you know Louise would eat strawberry ice cream twenty-four hours a day if she could, you are going to suggest that the cook share that she will serve Louise some strawberry ice cream for breakfast every day to help her medications go down. You might also suggest for the cook to share that they can probably take a healthier route and get her to drink a strawberry Fairlife shake with forty-two grams of protein mixed in. Either way, your community's cook has a plan for how to get her back on track with her medications.

The real differentiator here is that those team members, who are the experts in their departments, are getting involved in her care *before she's even decided to move in.* They are laying out a plan and describing what a solution could look like before she's even made a move-in commitment. At the same time, they're giving Louise and Angela a glimpse of what living here would be like. All of these sincere caring efforts can lift so much burden and worry off of the families' shoulders and help them feel so much better.

WHEN THE PLAN HAS TO PIVOT

While planning is essential on the tour, sometimes you have to turn on a dime and change your plan for the tour. If you're walking along past the nurses' area and the mailboxes and the beauty shop and a prospective resident asks, "Who comes and does everyone's hair here?" that's a trigger to learn more. This woman sounds like someone who gets her hair done a lot. You might want to ask some more questions about this. What kinds of hair services does she usually enjoy?

This is when you spontaneously decide to go with the flow. "Would you like to meet the hairdresser? It looks like she's free right now."

Most salespeople blow by the beauty shop and barely give the customer the time to wonder about it. They hit the dining room, memory care, and a couple of model rooms and then go back to the family room to try to close a sale.

You want to prioritize your customer's personal concerns by designing the tour based on what they express to you as important. Take them there first, otherwise they'll be preoccupied with wanting to see it the whole time and won't even be paying attention to what you do show them.

You should also take them to what they are interested in first because it can alleviate any potential obstacles. If you don't address their top of mind concerns early on, a minor obstacle can turn into a much bigger one, all because you didn't address it. If they told you ten times that room style will be a big sticking point with their mom and instead of going there first, you chose to spend the whole tour talking about the delicious food and the arts and crafts area, don't be surprised if they don't come back. Next time, say, "It sounds like the first thing we need to establish here is whether the space we have available will meet your mom's needs. So let's see that first."

Helping the customer see those high priorities first also builds trust. It says to the customer that you understood what was important and why it was important to them. You two had a really good conversation about how Mom's curio cabinet could fit in this room with all of her lovely collectibles. If their dad is outdoorsy and they want to see the walking paths, but he is also likely to need memory care, you're going to explain that memory care suites have a secured patio with a walking path and a garden. You may also share that there is a gardening club that takes care of the flowers and vegetables. And on the outings your community offers, their "outdoorsy dad" will be walking out on lawns and in other park-like places.

DOORWAYS TO A SALE

I'm a big believer in shadow boxes outside the residents' rooms, for several reasons. You can say all day long that your community offers personalized care, that you have care managers who are consistently the same person so your dad can get to know them. He will be able to get very comfortable with the people that are going to help him with his bath and settle him in at night, make sure he's taking his medications, entice him to come to activities on a day that he's feeling down, but it's hard to see all those little but important things on a tour.

But if you show them the residents' various shadow boxes

as you walk down the halls of the community, they'll see the shadow boxes just outside each resident's room filled with trinkets and photos of things that are really important to that resident. In just a few seconds you get a glimpse of what matters to that resident.

Shadow boxes also help the caregivers get a quick glimpse of who this resident is as a human being before they step into their room to administer care. It gives the care manager who has just had a challenging interaction with another resident an opportunity to pause briefly before they enter the room and refocus on this resident, this person, and their particular life. They can go in more grounded and be more present and available when they ask if the resident is ready to take their bath. It cues that caregiver that this person is more than the problems they are encountering as they age. They've lived a full and wonderful life.

The subtle message that the shadow box sends is that this place cares about every unique individual, and this absolutely builds trust that they will be treated with the same kind of individualized tailored attention if they decide to live here.

Personalizing the current residents' doorways should be a value and priority in your community. This is one of the few things that most communities, but not all, do to demonstrate their care for each individual who lives there. If your community doesn't do a great job with this, and all the doorways have a little sign that says, "Welcome friends and family" and they're not tailored, then the prospective resident and their family are going to see them on the tour and feel as if they've been lied to. You will undermine their trust, because your website says that everyone here receives tailored attention. So something doesn't feel right here. Something doesn't jibe.

INVOLVING THE EXPERTS

It's these interactions with the team members that really make a huge difference. It's so much more valuable than showing them the activity room. Angela doesn't care about that. She cares about her mom taking her medications so she feels better.

In many ways, your job comes down to reassurance. Whether it's medications or incontinence or falling or wandering or any of the long list of common concerns with our aging family members, we have the opportunity, and the responsibility, to show people that we can help.

We can't promise that we'll be able to prevent things from happening, of course. We need to be our authentic self and tell the customer, "We cannot prevent your dad from falling. We can't anticipate when that might happen. But what we can do is have you talk with the head nurse of the community. You'll be talking to the person who manages all of the care managers who would take care of your dad. And you can have a conversation with them about how it is that we would work to best understand where those vulnerable moments could be.

If he falls often, and if what we learned when we were listening to learn is that a lot of his falls have happened in the middle of the night when he's had to get up to go to the bathroom, we will track that and understand that. Bill generally gets up at around two and five o'clock in the morning. Those are the times when he wakes up to go to the bathroom.

The care managers who provide daily care will get to know his habits and can then try to pre-empt a potential fall by checking in with the resident before he gets up to go to the bathroom. They will softly knock on the door, open the door, and if he seems restless, wake him up and ask how he's feeling, whether he has to go to the bathroom, and if there's anything else he needs. That is how we can build a process that hopefully will limit the potential falls. Anybody who says that they can keep people from falling is not telling the truth. But this kind of plan is one that is real and possible.

It's about having these kinds of genuine conversations. There won't be a camera spying on him twenty-four hours a day, but we can put a few nightlights in the room and make sure the path is clear to the bathroom.

When you are in the solution-building stage, you're making sure prospective residents and their families are meeting with the people who will execute what needs to be done to keep their Mom or Dad as healthy and safe as possible—and this is usually the nurse. These discussions with your customer and the nurse or other healthcare provider need to be very personalized, because when the prospective resident moves in, the solution has to be tailored to the senior's individual needs. How your community can help with their Mom's incontinence or Dad's Parkinson's all depends on the particulars of their medical concerns and needs, and it's going to be up to that nurse to help present a solution.

How can we make sure their mother doesn't have an accident with her new friends in the dining room? If you've learned that Mom is usually okay as long as she gets to the bathroom every couple of hours, then your community's nurse can reassure her that they'll check with her to see if she has to go before she goes down to the dining room. If she's already with a group, they might ask the group, "Does anybody here need to make a trip to the potty?" These things are built into the overall care plan. A trip to the dining room includes a trip to the bathroom.

The main thing is that inviting your customer to talk to the person who's actually going to be in charge of solving their problem will be a very different experience than what they'll have in most communities. Involving the team members will make all the difference for the customer and you as the salesperson.

This type of approach is rare as it takes coordination; when done well, you'll increase your closing ratio, as it will be significantly different from their experience with the competitors. This approach also will help the family member in the retelling of their experience. It may sound a little like this, "All three communities offered everything their Mom needs; however, at one community we actually sat down with the nurse, Jessica, and the chef, Brigitte, and talked through how they will work with their Mom to ensure she eats and takes her medication. It's a different experience."

Now the telling of the story to the other family members who you have to get on board with this major life decision includes the story of connecting with the actual care providers.

The sibling has already begun to form relationships with the very people who will be there solving any challenges that their parent is experiencing. It's not about whether they like you, their salesperson, or not. It's about whether they like the person who is actually going to take care of their parent. If they have a problem with their dad's care, they know who they'll need to call, and you need to try to make sure they feel good about that.

If you've gotten this far with the customer, it means your dining room forks are probably clean, and you've done your homework, preparing for a successful tour by finding ways to demonstrate all the ways your community offers all the things that tie to the customer's primary needs.

At the end of your tour, you are always going to clarify and recommend next steps. If those next steps are not in line with the customer's needs or abilities or stage of the process, then you need to rethink them, because you always need to be aligned with where they are in their buying journey.

Once the tour comes to an end and you've agreed to next steps with the prospective resident and their families, it's time to personalize the next phase: follow up. In the next chapter, we will look at how you can be creative and proactive in your follow up and manage the sales process in a way that leads to the outcome you want.

GET CURIOUS (IT TAKES PRACTICE)
EXERCISE: INVOLVING THE RIGHT EXPERT
Objective:

To identify and assign the appropriate community expert to sit down with a prospective resident or their family, based on the unique challenges or concerns they have shared.

Instructions:
Step 1: Identify the Resident's Challenges

- Reflect on your recent discovery conversations. What specific challenges or concerns have the prospective resident or their family shared with you?
  - Example: Does the resident have trouble taking medications? Are they concerned about dietary needs? Are they worried about social engagement or mobility issues?

Step 2: Match the Challenges to the Correct Expert

- **Nurse:**
  - Best suited for addressing clinical or health-related concerns, such as managing medications, preventing falls, or addressing mobility issues.

○ **Example:** If the prospective resident, like Louise in the scenario, isn't eating well and can't take medications on an empty stomach, the nurse would be the best person to discuss how medication schedules can be tailored and how care staff will help manage the situation.

- **Chef/Dining Services Coordinator:**
  ○ Ideal for concerns around diet, nutrition, or specialized meal plans.
  ○ **Example:** If the resident is reluctant to eat due to health conditions or food preferences, involve the chef to show how they can provide personalized meals that meet their needs and dietary preferences, like offering a strawberry shake to help with medication.
- **Programming Director:**
  ○ The right choice for discussing lifestyle preferences, hobbies, and engagement activities that keep the resident socially and mentally active.
  ○ **Example:** If the resident has been socially isolated or is looking for specific hobbies (like gardening, knitting, or playing cards), the programming director can show how they can offer activities tailored to the resident's interests.
- **Executive Director:**
  ○ Best for providing reassurance on the overall experience, operational questions, and decision-making concerns. They often carry authority and experience, making families feel confident in the leadership.
  ○ **Example:** If the family is concerned about the overall safety, security, or operations of the community, a conversation with the executive director will offer clarity on how the entire community works to keep their loved one safe and engaged.

Step 3: Craft Tailored Introductions

- Once you've identified the right expert, work on creating a personalized introduction. Communicate to the prospect how the expert will address their concerns specifically.
  - **Example:** "We know Louise loves strawberry ice cream, and since she's had trouble with her appetite, I've arranged for our chef, Brigitte, to meet with you both to explain how we can offer options that might appeal to her, like her favorite strawberry treats or a nutrition-packed smoothie."

Step 4: Conduct a Role-Play or Live Practice

- Practice pairing hypothetical resident scenarios with the right expert to build confidence.
  - **Scenario:** A resident has concerns about their memory care. Who do you connect them with? A nurse to discuss memory care strategies and safety protocols or the programming director to talk about engagement programs for memory care residents?

Step 5: Debrief the Exercise

- After making your expert recommendations, reflect on how the meeting went:
  - Did the expert offer valuable insights?
  - Did it help build trust with the prospective resident or family?
  - Was the expert's involvement aligned with the resident's primary concerns?

This exercise will help you think critically about who should be involved in a tour or meeting, ensuring the resident meets the most relevant team member. It also helps the family see the collaborative approach your community takes to addressing challenges.

Chapter 8

Tailor Your Follow Up

"You have to have confidence in your ability, and be tough enough to follow through."

—ROSALYNN CARTER

In the process of putting this book together, I have had the opportunity to hear and read many beautiful stories. I'll share just a few here that demonstrate how curiosity and genuine caring, especially when personalizing your follow-up, can make all the difference.

A couple who were considering a move to a senior living community came in to meet with Lynn, a sales director at a community in Pennsylvania. Lynn could tell that the gentleman, Richard, wanted to be anywhere else but at the community. You could also see that his wife, Dorothy, was very eager and looking forward to a possible move, which would allow them to focus on spending time doing more of what they love, versus keeping up with the demands of maintaining the family home.

They sat down to talk, and Lynn explained that this meeting was just for them to get a feel for what senior living offers. There was no pressure to make any decisions; she was just there to answer their questions. A few minutes into the conversation, she noticed that Richard had on a hunting hat. She asked Richard if he was a hunter, and he explained that he had been an avid hunter for many years but had not hunted in the past few years, and he really missed it.

Lynn shared that her husband also hunted, and that they had a cabin that her husband often used for hunting. When Lynn asked Richard what he missed most about hunting, he quickly answered, "Venison chili."

Dorothy chimed in that over the years, his hunting trips had been a time for her to just relax, read a book, see her girlfriends, and have some alone time as a "hunter's widow." Lynn genuinely understood what it meant to be a hunter's widow, and they were able to laugh and joke about it all. They spent a good half hour just discussing everything about hunting— where he hunted, what he preferred to hunt, and all that. Lynn could see by his smile that Richard was beginning to relax a bit.

At this point in the conversation, it became apparent to Lynn that they loved each other very much, and yet they also wanted to be able to enjoy their individual hobbies. Richard started asking questions about what there was to do in Lynn's community, which led to a discussion of the various men's groups offered there. When Richard and Dorothy were getting ready to leave, Lynn asked if she could come by their house to answer any additional questions and bring a calendar of events being held at the community during the upcoming months.

Lynn made that home visit, and not only did she bring venison chili for Richard, she also delivered a small ladies relaxation basket with teas, a journal, candle, and candy. As of this writing, the gentleman who originally thought he would never move into a senior living community has attended several different events there with his wife, and they are currently on the waiting list for a two-bedroom apartment in the community. He always gives Lynn a huge hug when he sees her.

I met Fabrienne, a director of sales at a community who was working with a prospective resident named Karen. Fabrienne had learned that one of Karen's hobbies was to grow flowering plants that others might find difficult to grow. One in particular was the double oriental lily "Anouska," which has snow-white petals with a bubblegum pink tint around the edges. Fabrienne was genuinely interested in these flowers and took to doing some research. She learned that this variety rarely produces pollen, so they don't produce fertile seeds, and this makes them harder to propagate. Fabrienne realized these flowers took a lot of understanding to grow and nurture. When I was there, we brainstormed ways to demonstrate to Karen that she had been seen and heard. How could we take what Fabrienne had learned about Karen's love for these flowers and do something special for her as part of our follow up?

Fabrienne dug more deeply into these beautiful flowers. She found a website that featured a how-to guide on growing Anouskas.

She recommended a home visit as a next step and chose to have the community nurse come along to better understand the medical challenges Karen was having at home. Karen agreed, and they set a time for the end of the week. Even though the next step was agreed upon, that did not keep Fabrienne from sending a personalized follow-up note. The note went something like this: "Thank you for meeting with me earlier today. After you left, I had a few minutes to learn more about the flowers we discussed. It sounds like caring for them is pretty complicated. I can't wait to see them when we visit with you in a few days. I did find this website in my search and thought you would enjoy looking at some of the articles and photos."

I'm sure you can guess how this ultimately worked out.

During pre-sales at another community I once supported, we needed to increase deposits, so we set a goal to find ways to create experiences for customers to experience what life would be like for residents once we opened. Joanne, a prospective resident, had visited the pre-open space several times with her family, and the salesperson had made a home visit. Still, she was hesitant to select a suite and make a deposit.

During discovery, the salesperson Jackie had learned Joanne loved to cook for her family and over the years had perfected an Italian pasta sauce. It was her signature dish she always made for holidays. Jackie met with the chef, and they decided to invite her to share this special recipe. The chef made a call to Joanne asking if she would mind teaching him how to make this special pasta sauce that he had heard so much about, and she agreed.

The chef then arranged for several of the cooks on his team to join in on the lesson. Joanne arrived and joined them in the kitchen to prepare the sauce. While they were all cooking, they sang Italian songs and swapped family holiday stories. A good time was had by all, and Joanne later left with a few mason jars of her pasta sauce and a very big smile on her face.

The following week, Jackie bought one of those cards that you can record a personal message in and the message plays when it's opened. The chef and cooks recorded themselves singing a few verses of one of the songs they all sang together that day while cooking Joanne's sauce into the card, and then Jackie sent it to Joanne as a thank you card for sharing her recipe.

When Joanne received this card, she was moved by the thoughtfulness of it. She later shared that listening to the singing card brought not only a memory to her mind but also put a smile on her face. As a result of all of this highly tailored follow up, she moved in several months earlier than she'd originally planned and spent a bit more than she had anticipated.

I hope as you read the stories above you can see that all three of these salespeople were very purposeful in learning more about the customer than just their immediate needs, current challenges, and financial situation. All of these stories support the "slow down to go fast" theory in sales. Ask more questions and focus on the person sitting in front of you.

What made these three sales journeys so effective was the personalization, and the key takeaway here is that following up effectively requires just as much personalization as the tour.

How do we help prospective residents and their families get to that feeling of "Yes, I belong here"? It all has to be very conscious on our part (even though it's really not so conscious on their part—but that's okay, because this is your job, not theirs). As we've seen, one way to consciously help them feel they belong in your community is to personalize your follow up after the tour. Follow up, when tailored, strengthens the trust between the customer and salesperson by clearly demonstrating "We hear you and we see you."

Regardless of where customers are in their journey, follow up is another opportunity to differentiate yourself from everyone else. If you have a customer who has toured more than one community (which is most common since people usually look at three to five places), they have probably seen similar amenities and learned about similar programs and options for care. How do you make a difference?

The difference we've been discussing is an approach filled

with moments that matter. Moments based on what you've learned and moments that will demonstrate that you listened and that you see them as a unique individual. Just like the quote in *Field of Dreams*, "If you build it, they will come," you can think, "If you ask them, they will tell you." What they tell you will help you support them through to the end of this very difficult decision-making process.

After each tour a customer takes, it is likely that their salesperson will follow up. This might be a phone call to "check in" with them or to find out how their mom is doing, or it might be that they send an email or leave a voice message. However it's delivered, the customer will experience a follow-up action. In my view, follow up is an opportunity to put an exclamation point on everything you've done so far and to continue to give them a glimpse of what life will feel like when they live in your community.

To put an exclamation point on it all, you won't call them and ask, "How's your mom?" Instead, you can ask, "How did the conversation go with your brother?" or "Is your brother still planning to come to town next week?"

Once again, you are using what you have learned and tying it back to what your community offers. You want to remind them of the ways in which it felt different in your community.

For instance, if you're curious about the role her brother would play in making the decision and you were able to provide specific information for her to use in the discussion with him, then now, you are going to continue to take that high level of interest and not just give them some kind of canned follow-up messaging, like, "Thank you so much for visiting with us on Tuesday. We really enjoyed meeting you and your father. Please know that we would love to continue to be a resource for you."

Instead you will seek to understand if the information you provided was helpful when she spoke with her brother. You can now take the opportunity to learn even more by asking, "What will be most important for your brother to learn when he tours the community next week?" Then you can move on to building a tailored visit for her brother.

If it's appropriate, you should also consider doing a home visit as part of your follow up. As sales professionals, we need to understand how much a home visit can aid in continued discovery. In my opinion, this is an underutilized next step. An afternoon with the prospective resident in their home can lead to a new perspective on how they currently spend their time. You become privy to a treasure trove of visual discovery, through seeing photos of their family, how the home is maintained, and all of the evidence of what brings the customer joy.

Whatever your next step is, it bears repeating that it needs to be highly personalized and tailored to where the customer is in their decision-making process.

GET CREATIVE WITH YOUR FOLLOW UP

It's important to bring imagination and creativity to the follow up and to tie the follow up to something that is specific to something you learned. It's even better when it's something that you learned that may be aligned with something other than just care.

For example, if you have learned that a prospective resident is having a tough time managing her diabetes, you may want to jump directly to how her diabetes will be managed at your community. And this makes sense because you discovered a problem and you provided a solution. However, what might you have learned if you asked just a few more questions, and how would what you learned have aided in differentiating your community through tailored follow up?

Those questions might sound like this: "How are you currently managing your diabetes? When do you tend to see the rise in your sugar? Is there anything specific you really enjoy to eat after dinner? Sounds like you make a terrific strawberry rhubarb pie! How have you altered the recipe so it has less sugar?

You do need to demonstrate to the customer that you can care for her mom or dad's diabetes. But you also need to demonstrate to her that the prospective resident will still enjoy dessert. This could be a great opportunity to pull the chef into your follow-up strategy. You might say, "The chef would like to meet with you. He would like to share some of the things that they do to make sure we're serving delicious meals that will meet your needs as a diabetic. Our chef would like to try to make a version of your strawberry rhubarb pie that is diabetic-friendly and get your opinion. Would you mind sharing your recipe?"

This strategy combines both the care and the happy lifestyle outside of the care in a way that both bases are covered.

She's not moving in to bake a pie. She is moving in because she can't take care of her diabetes. But in the process, we don't want her to lose the joy of baking pies. So as a challenge, the chef makes a sugar-free version of her recipe. "I think it would be really great when you come in for the assessment if you could bring your pie, and we'll do a kind of taste test challenge between your pie and the chef's version of your pie."

A few things happen when you deploy a follow-up strategy like the one above; you acknowledge she needs to have support managing her diabetes, that she loves baking, and that she is especially proud of her strawberry rhubarb pie. With this information, you've been able to introduce her to the chef and invited her to challenge him on replicating one of her beloved recipes. Imagine how that would feel to someone who is looking at such a huge life change due to an inability to manage her diabetes. Here she has been treated with dignity and respect versus being treated as someone with something that needs to be fixed.

"Cooking up" a plan like this takes creativity on your part. But the challenge for you, the salesperson, is to create a follow-up experience that is twofold. It satisfies the requirement that we meet their healthcare needs, and it satisfies the recommended sales strategy of appealing to the person's happiness by also taking care of things that bring the prospective resident joy.

When you can partner those two things, the results are powerful.

Another way to go could be introducing her to members of the baking club that meets every Wednesday. "What would you think about coming in next Wednesday? I think they are going to make some pies and are having a pie tasting contest. Why don't you make your regular pie, and our chef will make the same recipe but a version that is diabetic friendly?" These are just examples. There are a thousand things you can do, but the important thing is to figure out an experience that will show your customers that they are seen and heard throughout the entire sales process, which likely results in a profound feeling of mattering. And don't we all want to feel like we matter?

Even if they say no, because they can't make the pie-off happen, just the fact that we acknowledged that the clinical needs and the emotional needs are equally important will appeal to the customer. They are coming to live here because while everyone can manage their diabetes, your community is the only one that has demonstrated that they can address their psychological needs.

Any senior living community can help them with physical things they can no longer do at home anymore. But when you can partner that with things that will continue to bring them joy, continue to give them opportunities to learn things, and continue to give them opportunities to make friends, all of the things that bring us joy, not only is that the right thing to do, it is also by far the biggest differentiator.

If you hold those two things as equal, you will stand out.

Let's say a customer has fairly well-progressed Alzheimer's disease Still, if she is a person who used to grow amazing flowers, and you found that out because you were curious and you listened to learn, you can take the steps to have those exact kind of flowers delivered to her, even if they are artificial or if it is just a card with a painting of those flowers. It shows respect and gives her dignity, and that has value beyond money.

You just have to be willing to go the extra step.

If it was your mom who was moving in, and you couldn't take care of her anymore because she'd become combative and difficult to manage, and a salesperson helped you bring in a picture of the flowers to put in her room and helped your mom remember that these are the same kind of flowers she used to grow, how would you feel?

Every human being deserves to have someone to understand what brings them joy and to try to facilitate that in one way or another. Even if it is just saying, "Come to the gardening club and teach us how to grow these ridiculously persnickety, hard-to-grow flowers."

Think beyond the "traditional" follow-up actions. For example, inviting a prospective resident back to participate in a random activity that they haven't expressed interest in or inviting them back for lunch or an assessment is not creative. It's not that any of these are necessarily wrong. It's just that if they are not tied to a particular, unique need the customer has; it won't evoke the desired emotion from the customer. And that emotion is *I feel seen and heard. I feel like my stories matter, and I think this is a place where I would fit in and belong.* This is exactly how it should feel when someone is making such a huge life-changing decision.

Take a moment, right now, and consider one of the prospective residents you are currently working with. Write down three to five things you know about them and brainstorm your next follow-up step. If it's exactly the same step you've taken with another prospective resident, try again. Keep in mind, this follow-up action is specific to this prospective resident and tailored in a way that gives a glimpse of what their care will be like in your community.

If you are stumped, think of the prospective resident as a resident already living in your community. Consider what you've learned about their needs and what would happen in your community to meet that need. Now you can create a follow-up step unlike anything your competition will consider, and one that will wow your prospective resident. If this person moves in, send me a note! I'd love to hear about it.

Traditional follow-up actions taken with senior living customers are generally the same between competitors, which is great news for you! With some creativity and effort, you can differentiate yourself through your actions, based on what you've learned through your curiosity-driven questions and patient listening.

LET YOUR CURIOSITY SHINE IN FOLLOW UP

Traditional follow up tends to fall into three categories: an assessment, an opportunity to meet with or talk with a department coordinator, or inviting a customer to a group activity or onsite event. These can all be somewhat tailored but are likely very similar to what your competition is recommending as well.

If you have laid the groundwork through Curiosity-Driven Sales that has enabled you to show the customer what it will feel like to live in your community, then they can sense that they will feel seen and heard and understood. They can sense that the team members are genuinely interested, and the chef wants to know how they can best meet the residents' needs. The way you have interacted with your customers has demonstrated how they will be treated if they decide to move in.

The follow up, then, is simply another reminder that you've been curious and shown genuine interest in their mom or dad. You're curious about all of the specifics, beyond just medical issues and which suite will best fit their needs. These are important, of course, but the more you can demonstrate that you have listened by tailoring the follow up specifically to each individual customer, the larger the gap will grow between you and your competition.

The salesperson is in the driver's seat at this point because, whether this whole process took them four days or four months, they understand the customer to a degree that they know what is most important to them. They know what will bring them joy and what will help them live their best life.

"If you take the apartment on the first floor," you say, "you'll be able to put the bird feeder out there, and you mentioned you love to sit in the morning and have your cup of tea and watch the birds. I think that suite would really fit your needs."

This is a time to talk about things that will meet their needs and the things they like to do. You are already armed with information to add, all of the things you looked at together, and the things you know they don't want to miss out on. You have all your notes in the CRM that you entered after every interaction that all adds up to the story of this buyer's process. You've gone back to it and taken a second look to help you personalize your follow up.

Your curiosity has been purposeful as you've worked to pull out of that customer some unique facts that you are going to be able to leverage in the sales process. Your ability to be a Nosy Nellie was not for nothing. It was out of respect for your customer and the need to know things in order to help them through this time of transition.

Follow up has to happen after every interaction. However, as we've seen all along the way, the type of follow up and the delivery method of that follow up depends on what the customer needs and where they are in their decision-making process. Let's delve into that a little more as we think about following up.

TAILORING COLD, WARM, AND HOT LEADS

The goal in sales is always to create a compelling reason for the customer to move on to the next step. But just as importantly, this recommended next step needs to be aligned with where the customer is in their decision-making journey. Understanding their timing is an aspect of personalizing your follow up that cannot be overlooked.

The "best next step" the customer needs to take may not align with your need to close a sale, but it's important that you set your needs aside at this point and focus on *their needs*. If you're not tuned into what the customer needs, it creates a disconnect that often leads to an obstacle you'll then need to overcome. This is an obstacle that may not have been thrown in your path if you had just taken a few moments to consider the customer's state of mind and identify where they are in their decision-making journey.

When somebody is in the hospital, they have to make an immediate decision. That's a hot lead, and it's always going to be your immediate priority. But as we've discussed, those kinds of sales are only ten percent of all your move-ins. The vast majority happen much slower, and these warm and cold leads will still increase your numbers, so these customers need to be nurtured just as much as the hot leads. You need to stay with them on their buying journey every step of the way—from the first phone call to helping them decide on a room and then moving forward at a natural pace with the deposit. We're not talking about the emergency, where you're saying, "We have a suite, and you can move in Thursday." This is more of a medium-length process. It's longer and more drawn out because they're not in total desperation and they have time to drag their feet, and so, of course, they do.

After the tour, for these warm and cold leads, the next step you recommend may be a home visit, a visit with a group of residents already living in the community, an outing, a meeting off site, or even an assessment. Whatever it is, what matters most is that the follow up offered must meet the customer where they are in the decision-making process—and (in case I have not said it already) not necessarily where you are in the sales process!

Lean in to your creativity, learn from your curiosity, and offer the customer a next step that is so highly tailored to them and their situation that they can't resist agreeing to your recommendation.

Not everyone is willing to share personal information before the tour. Sometimes you don't even start learning the deep information about what they really need and what brings them joy until after the tour. Perhaps they've been resistant to your curiosity until they come in. But at a certain point, hopefully you feel comfortable saying something like, "If you wouldn't mind, I'd love to just hear a little bit more about her life both past and present. What did she do for work, or did she have the opportunity to stay home and focus on the family?"

"Can you tell me about your family? Does she have any siblings?"

"How has her experience been living alone, and how long has she been on her own?"

"How long have you been involved in caring for her, and how has that journey been for you?"

MEET THEM OFF-SITE

There are plenty of opportunities after the tour to continue your follow up. It's not rare to have customers visit the community two or three times before they make a buying decision. This means you can keep getting insights into their unique individuality. Home visits in particular can go a long way toward helping with this.

During a training a few years ago focusing on follow up, I took the role of the customer in a role-playing exercise. One of the trainees kept wanting me to come into the community as the next step. I, as the customer, kept saying, "I haven't talked to my mom about this yet, and I'm not comfortable coming into the community until I do." The salesperson stayed dedicated to creating compelling reasons for me to tour without success.

He then offered this suggestion: "I know there's a Starbucks right around the corner from where you work. Why don't I meet you for a coffee? I'll have some information on my laptop I can show you to give you some ideas as to what it might be like so you can feel a little better about talking to your mom when the time comes." I said "yes" to this recommended next step. We can often get hung up on what *we need* and don't take a moment to consider what the customer may need.

It doesn't matter if it makes no sense for a customer to refuse a tour. That's our problem, not theirs. We need to find the way forward and consider what the customer needs at this time. The old adage of "If you could just see how special we are, once you do you'll understand what is so very different about us" does not work for everyone, and sticking to what we feel is the right next step can create even more objections throughout the sales process.

In my experience, off-site visits are not leveraged enough. We've discussed meeting the customer where they are in the process, so why not do this physically as well as mentally. It may take a bit of courage and creativity, but the benefit of meeting where the customer is most comfortable can lower defenses, and, as a result, you'll learn more. Also, arranging a meeting off-site sends a message that you acknowledge their hesitation yet still want to provide the information needed at this time in the decision-making process. If they are not ready to come to you, you can go to them. This is a critical part of follow up—to be somewhat flexible around where and how your follow up happens.

If you're committed to learning more about them and committed to helping them to know you care, then be willing to go to them. When a customer has yet to commit, and you are still willing to put what they need first, this is a way to demonstrate your brand promise and what life will be like in your community.

You are demonstrating that you are here to care for them as much as you are for their loved one. Those making this difficult decision also need support and affirmation during the process.

As a salesperson, you have key performance indicators and metrics that, when met, increase the likelihood of meeting specific goals. At times, our need to meet the KPIs conflicts with what a customer may need to move forward in the decision-making process. Here's an example: You need to complete six community tours with customers each week. It's Wednesday and you've conducted four community tours with prospective residents and their families. You've been working with a family who has yet to tour. You are not sure why they are hesitating, and you believe the next step should be a visit to the community. With pressure mounting, you decide to connect with the family and push harder for them to tour.

You say and do all of the things you've been taught to create a compelling reason to tour, but deep down you know you need two more tours this week. From the customer's perspective, you are no longer seeking to understand their hesitation; you are insisting on what "you" need. So now you've made this call, and the family does not agree to your recommended next step, and you still do not understand the hesitation. You've created a gap between being focused on what the customer needs and what you want to happen.

This approach rarely works and can result in a silent retreat from the customer. Suddenly they are not calling you back or answering your emails. Another approach might have been to focus on finding out more about the family dynamics, acknowledging that taking action can be unsettling and feel like a betrayal. It's one thing to talk about a solution—it's another to actually take action.

UNSELFISH ADVANCES

I would encourage you to be unselfish in creating your advances. Put the customer's needs first and you are more likely to ensure ongoing engagement that will result in a move-in. This again is that "slow down to go fast" theory. Being an advocate for the customer is not just something that sounds good. When you seek to understand the authenticity of your actions, it will set you apart from the competition even more. This is what my consulting partner, Jessica Phaup, coined an "unselfish advance." It's acknowledging that the customer needs something more from us before they can move forward emotionally toward making a decision and making an effort to give them that.

When you focus your customer interactions on learning as much as you can and staying aligned with where they are in the decision-making process in the environment where they are most comfortable, it may feel like you are slowing down. Some people might refer to it as "not taking control of the conversation," but the reality is you will speed up your outcomes. Sound counterintuitive? Maybe. I'd like to remind you that only 10 percent of inquiries result in a move-in; wouldn't you like a chance to win more often with the other 90 percent? Try slowing down.

Just because you need another tour doesn't mean that the customer is ready to come in and tour. Just because you need a move-in doesn't mean they'll move in tomorrow.

Managers, experts, and supervisors will likely focus on your metrics. It's not that they don't understand that those metrics actually represent people; it's just an easier way to forecast success. When all your supervisor wants to know is who's moving in tomorrow or who's moving in this week, be careful not to fall into the trap of only talking to people who can maybe move in this week. It's not that your supervisors want you to ignore any customers, but they are most interested in celebrating the work you did that resulted in today's tour and today's move-in.

A wiser method is to balance your time between customers with urgent needs and customers who are not yet ready. Here's a secret: there is nothing you can do to make someone ready to make a senior living buying decision. There is a lot you can do to guide a customer through the decision-making process, therefore influencing their decision through creating a thoughtful and tailored path on which to move forward based on recommendations that make sense to your customer. You can do things that increase the urgency of your customer making a buying decision, but staying aligned with your customers will increase the number of them who advance to a buying decision.

This focus on slowing down and improving the quality of your engagement by personalizing interactions is a differentiator that will put you ahead of your competition every time. That "rushed, get it today" mindset exists for all senior living salespeople, so while your competition is focused on what they need to close a sale *now*, you'll find that you have more customers making the buying decision. Why? Because the interactions with you and the community team at every step gave a view of what life will be like in your community— thoughtful, caring and interested, all the while providing great care.

Understanding how to manage people in your sales funnel

and tailoring your behavior to their unique situation are what professional sales work is all about.

Treva, a tenured senior living salesperson, had courted a prospect, Beverly, for several years as she was considering a move to independent living at her community. She was successful in creating compelling reasons for Beverly to visit the community, she invited her to events in which she learned Beverly would have interest, and Beverly had agreed to several home visits and had even gone on a bus trip with current residents to see the fall leaves. Clearly this salesperson was doing all of the right things to stay connected during the decision-making process. Treva then invited Beverly for a three-day complimentary stay during the month of December. She also invited her dog Shadow to come along. When Beverly arrived, they had the room all decked out for the holidays with a Christmas tree and gifts under the tree for both Beverly and even a stocking full of doggie treats and a Christmas sweater for Shadow.

On the third day of this stay, Treva asked Beverly what was holding her back from making the move. Beverly acknowledged what a fun three days she had just experienced and said she felt more rested than she had in a long time and had a lot of fun making new friends. Her reply was that she had two pets—Shadow, whom she absolutely could not part with—and a cat named Jelly Bean, whom she couldn't just abandon.

Jelly Bean was what one might call an "outdoor cat," meaning that although he did spend time in the house, he spent much of his time in the yard, terrorizing the birds who faithfully spent time at her bird feeders. Not having access to come and go as he pleased would be too tough of an adjustment for Jelly Bean. Treva started looking around for a home for Jelly Bean, with the help of others on her team, and they found a perfect home with one of the care managers who had another "outdoor cat" and could provide the right living situation for Jelly Bean.

Treva coordinated the visits with Jelly Bean and his new family so that Beverly felt comfortable. She was able to meet the person her cat was going to live with and know he was going to a good loving home. For many years after Beverly moved in, Treva continued to get updates and pictures of Jelly Bean, showing how well he was doing, and she shared these with Beverly.

Sometimes, as was the case with Jelly Bean, you have to work a little harder as a salesperson. And sometimes you have to challenge yourself to build enough rapport in that very first brief phone call to learn really fascinating things, such as the fact that she used to design furniture or he used to be a concert pianist. The idea is to find ways you can do more than just show them around the community on the tour.

If you've followed all the steps outlined in the previous chapters, you have a road map you can use to get to this point. If you have done all the steps suggested, you will limit road-blocks, otherwise known as objections. Said another way, if you and the customer are on the same road, heading in the same direction at the right speed, you'll find the destination, your community, will become a pretty crowded place as the destination of choice.

Most of all, if you've appealed to your customer in a way that doesn't treat it like any other sales process—they're not buying a car or looking for a place to watch their puppy, after all—you have hopefully found a way to take a difficult sale and bring to it that piece of humanity that it deserves.

All along the way you have stayed in line with what they need. You have continuously and consistently been hunting for their pain points, their hopes and dreams, the things that light their fires that you can provide, and the things that extinguish their flames that they won't find in your community.

Using the results of your curiosity, you have designed an experience for them that feels good and makes sense for them. You are clearly aware of who they are as unique individuals, or you would not have been successful. Finally, you've paced the sales process appropriately, staying tuned in to where they are and how you can meet them in the moment.

Now it is time to tie their follow-up experience to some specific things you've learned along the way. Not everyone has the opportunity to create a singing card that will recollect a marvelous cooking experience, but not everybody needs that. So just as you've tailored the tour to them, you'll tailor the follow up to something you sense would not only reassure the customer about the care you can provide but also help them see that your community will go the extra mile to bring them joy.

To position yourself in a way that demonstrates that this decision will create opportunities to make new friends, learn new hobbies, share a beloved hobby, and maybe even gain back some of their independence, you must be your authentic self. No one's buying what you're selling unless it feels authentic and is coming from a place of genuine caring.

Is what you learn in sales training a comprehensive guide to selling senior living? Likely. The key is finding a way for you to execute on learned sales strategies in a way that your authentic self shines through. In the next chapter, we will take a look at the reasons why and the strategies you can use to maintain genuine connections with your authentic self.

GET CURIOUS (IT TAKES PRACTICE)
EXERCISE: CREATING MEMORABLE
MOMENTS THAT MATTER

Objective: Help salespeople deepen their understanding of prospective residents and families by identifying meaningful details and using them to create tailored, memorable follow-up actions that demonstrate the customer matters.

Step 1: Reflect on What You've Learned

- Take a moment to write down everything you've learned about the prospective resident and their family during the initial interactions, tours, or meetings. This includes:
  - **Personal Interests and Hobbies:** Have they shared anything they love to do, such as gardening, cooking, or attending concerts?
  - **Memories and Traditions:** What life events or traditions hold special meaning for them?
  - **Challenges:** What specific struggles or concerns do they face, such as health issues or emotional worries about moving into a new environment?
  - **Relationships:** What did they share about their relationships with family, friends, or pets?

Step 2: Analyze and Prioritize

- Look at what you've written down and prioritize the top two to three details that stand out the most in terms of emotional significance. These are often the details that speak to the heart of who the person is and what they value.
- For example, if a resident mentions that they used to bake with their grandchild every weekend or that they miss

tending to their rose garden, these are important personal details that can inform your follow-up strategy.

Step 3: Craft Your Memorable Moment

- Now, think about how you can incorporate these meaningful details into a memorable follow-up action. Consider actions that connect directly with their interests and emotions. The goal is to create a moment that reflects that you *listened* and *care* about what makes them unique.
- **Examples:**
  - **The Gardener:** Send them a small plant or flowers they used to grow. Attach a note that says, "I remember how much you loved gardening. We would love to show you our garden club, and maybe you can share some of your gardening tips with the residents."
  - **The Music Lover:** If they mentioned loving a particular band or type of music, send a music-related gift, like a CD or playlist of their favorite songs. Include a message: "We'd love to play some of your favorite songs when you visit us next time."
  - **The Baker:** If they love baking, set up a baking day with the chef at your community. The chef could recreate their favorite recipe, and you could follow up with a card saying, "Our chef would love to bake your famous pie with you. When can we set that up?"

Step 4: Tailor the Delivery

- How you deliver this moment matters as much as the moment itself. Consider ways that will have the most impact:

- Hand-delivering a gift with a personal note.
- Sending a tailored video message where you reference the meaningful detail.
- Inviting them back to the community to join a resident activity related to their passion (gardening, cooking, book club, etc.).

Step 5: Document the Experience

- After the follow up is completed, document everything in your CRM or notes so that you can build on it. Make sure to track how the prospect reacted, what touched them, and whether it led to a deeper conversation or the next step in their decision-making process.

Step 6: Reflect and Adjust

- After executing the tailored follow up, reflect on what worked and what could be improved. Did the moment resonate emotionally with the prospect? How did they respond? Use this to guide future interactions.

Step 7: Follow Up Thoughtfully

- After creating this memorable moment, keep the conversation going with thoughtful follow-up questions and actions that build on it. For instance:
  - "Did you have a chance to enjoy the flowers we sent? We'd love to hear how they're doing."
  - "When would you like to come in and bake that pie together? Our chef is excited to meet you."

Step 8: Be Genuine

- Always ensure that your actions are driven by a genuine interest in the person. The purpose of this exercise is to make sure that the prospect feels *seen, heard, and valued*— that they matter not just as a prospective resident, but as a human being with a rich life story.

This exercise aims to encourage sales professionals to dig deep into the personal details they learn from customers, making their follow-up actions far more meaningful and emotionally resonant. Creating moments that reflect genuine care and personalized attention helps build trust, and when customers feel they matter, they are far more likely to lean toward your solution.

Chapter 9

Authenticity

"Authenticity is the daily practice of letting go of who we think we're supposed to be and embracing who we are."

—BRENÉ BROWN

Most people do not equate sales with authenticity. In fact, a lot of times, the connotation of selling is the exact opposite of authenticity. After all, you're framing your product in the most positive light, strategically positioning it to fit the needs of your customer, and this takes some forced effort. So how can you reconcile your sales tactics with being your authentic self?

The gift of earning enough trust to find out what the customer cares about most, misses most, and celebrates most is your reward from listening to learn. So what does bringing your authentic self to your sales practice mean? Aren't I always "myself"? The answer to this is yes and no. I've seen some sales professionals get so caught up in always executing what they've learned in sales training that it impacts the way they interact with customers.

According to an article in *Psychology Today*, authenticity is "acknowledging and expressing our genuine thoughts, feelings, and beliefs." It's about being true to ourselves, even when it contradicts societal expectations or norms. As Glennon Doyle writes in *Untamed*, "Being human is not hard because you're doing it wrong; it's hard because you're doing it right."

Authenticity might feel like just an abstract concept, but there are tangible things you can do to be authentic in this work:

- Have a genuine understanding of what your community can and cannot do.
- Be comfortable in your own skin talking about really difficult things
- Be nimble enough to meet the customer where they are in their sales journey
- Don't try to be someone or something you're not

The most important thing you can do in the sales process to be your authentic self is to get to the point where you fully understand the product that you're selling, soup to nuts. You need to understand all the programs that your community offers. In order for you to have that alignment, you have to have deep knowledge about many things. You have to understand how your community manages diabetes and whether you have menus that fit a diabetic diet. How does your community help bed bound residents with late-stage Alzheimer's disease?

If you are familiar with "FAB"—which stands for Feature, Advantage, Benefit—you can personalize how a specific program will benefit the prospective resident. You can create statements with the F and A ahead of time, but the B is always personalized in a way that can be presented as "And what that means for you and/or your dad is…"

Think of it like this. Feature represents "what it is," and Advantage is "what it does." Once you can comfortably describe your programs and services, only then can you clearly share with a customer how that service or program will meet their needs.

Let's go back to "outdoorsy Dad." In that example, the Feature is the secured patio with walking paths and a garden, the Advantage is that residents can spend time outdoors safely, and in this example, the Benefit is "What that means for your dad is that he can spend time outside walking and getting his hands dirty in the garden, which you've shared is so very important to him, while still being in a safe and secured environment."

Understanding your programs and services allows you to advise someone who is considering living there in an accurate and thorough way. It also allows you to talk about it in a comfortable, natural way. This is the critical piece when it comes to authenticity. Through deep knowledge and understanding of the inner workings of what you are selling, you can clearly articulate that to the client, which will ensure that everything you say is authentic. Otherwise, you're just fumbling around in half-certainty or, worse, sharing misinformation.

If you can't answer all of their questions or give them all of the information they need, it will most likely just validate the assumption so many people have that all salespeople are shifty. Shiftiness is the opposite of authenticity. This is why being authentic in this role requires having a genuine understanding of your community and what it can and what it cannot offer them.

You also can't make promises that you can't deliver on if you want to be authentic. You can't say you can give the customer a price before the assessment is done if the assessment drives the price. You can, however, explain the daily room rates to give them an idea of the range and why it's so important to have an assessment completed. Because you know your facts, you can say these things, or not say things, with confidence. This confidence helps you exude authenticity and inspire confidence in your customer because they know they are being given all of the information they need to make the best decision.

The reality of this situation is that your customer is in a hard place. That is the reality, and pretending like it's not hard is a sure pathway to inauthenticity. For this reason, not only do you need to be comfortable in your own skin and comfortable in your extensive knowledge of the community, but you also need to be comfortable talking about uncomfortable things—things like their mom not making it to the toilet in time or their dad's confusion about what day it is and which town he's in.

Questions about dietary restrictions are much less personal and invasive than incontinence and memory loss, but still stressful to discuss. Although they are not quite as messy as toilet troubles and mental decline, they often have serious medical underpinnings that are just as difficult. For example, most senior living communities don't keep a kosher kitchen. For some families, that can be a deal-breaker, and it most certainly can be an awkward moment. They have to admit that they have religion-based dietary restrictions, and sometimes there is a stigma against that. But you can't let that awkwardness get in the way of your goal of helping this person find senior living that works well for them. If your customer needs kosher meals, but you don't offer kosher meals, you'll need to share that with them, and then you can share your solution. Your solution may sound like, "However, we do work with a service that delivers pre-packaged kosher meals." Of course, this is only if you already work with a service like that. If you don't already work with a service, you need to be completely transparent about that, even though you may risk losing the move-in.

Many communities don't offer gluten-free diets, and their salespeople will skirt around that subject, because they don't want to lose a sale. You need to be comfortable saying things like, "Our kitchen doesn't operate in a way that allows us to truly provide a gluten-free diet. There is bread being made near where the vegetables are being cooked. However, we can certainly advise you on which meals are going to have less gluten. We just don't serve a celiac-friendly diet here. Since your doctor wrote an order for that, I'm afraid we may not be a good fit for you."

You have to be brave enough to ask uncomfortable and very personal questions. You need to put everything on the table and be transparent. If they feel you are authentic and honest, and they sense that you are taking a genuine interest in them, they will be much more willing to trust you and give you all of the information you need to help them.

Authenticity builds rapport, and building rapport is a key component of any sales strategy. Building rapport lays the groundwork for discovery. Authentic rapport-building requires you, the salesperson, to lead with honesty and a genuine interest in the customer. Stay curious with your questions and temper any desire you may have to start sharing solutions. If you stay focused and listen to learn, not only will you learn more, you'll learn more than your competition will, which will allow you to share a more compelling solution when the time comes. A relationship built on trust will yield greater comfort on the part of the customer, which in return will earn you more robust answers to those "difficult" questions.

JUST BE YOU

How can you be anything other than "you"? Your greatest advantage in the sales process is you being you. Leaning into your natural tendencies and your unique personality will bring authenticity to your interactions. Here's an example: several years ago, I worked with a group of salespeople who were testing an evaluation that would enable them to quote an "estimated" cost of care. Want to show up as yourself and say and do things you would normally do. If you're not naturally funny (like I am—ha ha,) don't try to be funny. If you're not deep and serious in general when you're talking to people, don't get all deep and serious, unless it's completely warranted in the conversation.

The sad fact is we don't always act in ways that are in line with who we are as people. Sometimes we have to sacrifice aspects of that to get things done, or we have to push out of our comfort zone for any number of reasons. But if you understand the importance of knowing your product, knowing your prices, and knowing what needs to happen before this particular person can decide to move in, you become comfortable having all those discussions, and that is going to allow you to naturally evoke authenticity. If you are able to build a strong rapport, the customer is going to be much more willing and able to have the uncomfortable conversations with you. There's much less of a chance they will try to hide hard truths.

Imagine for a moment that a daughter has shared with you that her mother has no issues with her personal hygiene. She's having trouble remembering to take her medications, and she has a slightly shuffled gait, which has caused a couple of falls. But she has no issues getting to the bathroom in time.

Your community's nurse then visits the mother's house, and it is immediately obvious to her that the mother is not actually managing her personal hygiene very well. The nurse will come back to the community and say that the family didn't tell the truth. But in reality, it could be that the daughter just didn't feel comfortable disclosing that with you. She didn't feel comfortable enough to say, "No, that's not going well, and she won't wear Depends."

There are many other reasons why you might have been given false information by this daughter. The daughter may not have even known about her mother's difficulty with personal hygiene. Many times an adult child just won't describe a situation in the way that it's really happening. Embarrassment, shame, protection, all sorts of family dynamics come into play. There may be difficulties in the parent-child relationship. The elderly parent might not want to tell them the truth about difficult things. They'll keep secrets, or they might simply be in denial.

However, much of the time the adult child does know the state of their parents' abilities and just needs to feel comfortable enough that you are a real person, a genuinely caring person, in order to share some of these touchy subjects with you.

Hopefully you get to the point in your relationship where you say something like this:

"You know, the assessment is coming up, and the results will correlate with how much this will cost. So it would be great if I could understand as much as possible about what your mom can and cannot do. I'd like to go through a laundry list of questions based on all the things that we've been talking about, and if you're not sure, that's fine. We can just mark some answers as what you think is true, not what you know is true."

How you say it is up to you, but the important thing is to just be yourself as you navigate these tougher conversations.

You have come to be the kind of salesperson who knows how to be in your own skin while at the same time using your sales tactics. You need to balance appropriate social skills with being as down to earth as you can.

If you're sincerely trying to understand their problem, and it actually matters to you because you actually care, they will sense that. Let's face it, if you don't care, then that is a different problem—you might not be in the right job.

It is safe to assume that you work in senior living sales because you care about people at this stage of life and you have what it takes. You wouldn't be reading this book if you didn't. You value hard work, and that aligns with this job, because we all know it isn't easy. Working on mindfully being your authentic self with others and making genuine connections isn't easy. But if you do this work, your customers will sense it, and they will trust you. That, as you might imagine, will boost sales.

Everything depends on you remembering that a significant part of being a professional salesperson is knowing what you are selling and understanding what your community can and cannot do. If you are grounded in that when you are sharing information with families, then you will be at your most natural self—naturally! You won't be having to think about how to behave or how to say something because you'll have a sense of certainty about the information you're sharing.

To get there, you need to be almost constantly working on improving your understanding of what you are selling. How do you do this? You guessed it—through curiosity. You can bring the same curiosity you're bringing to the customer to your community's team. Be curious, and learn everything you can about your community. Above all else, this will help you give off that comfortable, confident glow of authenticity.

In the end, this is about asking yourself how you can

improve your level of comfort in the products that you're selling. It is also what will help you be quick on your feet, able to pivot on a dime, and meet the customer wherever they are in their journey.

STAY NIMBLE

Let's say a woman named Barbara calls you. Her mother is in a skilled nursing community because she broke her hip, and she's healed enough now that the skilled nursing community is going to discharge her imminently. She has too many stairs in her home to move back there, so she is in the very final stages of the senior living buying process.

They've flown over all the other steps and have zoomed to the end stage of the sales journey. They know nothing except for the discharge date, and they have to make a decision. In this situation, being authentic requires that you be nimble enough to understand what the daughter is going through and help her get through this as quickly as possible.

In that moment, you'll need to jump over many of the questions you might normally ask and move right to where the customer is in their decision-making. You are not going to ask what she likes to do or what she did for a living. That is beautiful when you can do it, but not when a customer comes to you at the end of their process and you have to dive right in. Eventually, you will still want to find ways to ask those other questions, because you want the prospective resident to live their best life when they move in. But in this situation, that has to come later.

If the daughter had come to you when her mom first broke her hip and was entering the hospital where she would be for a while and then rehab for weeks, you would have had time to leverage your curiosity in a holistic manner. This is not that situation. In a quick discharge situation, you can still be curious, but the curiosity should be around what is needed to meet the current care needs, the timing of the discharge, and how to support the family through the move-in process.

But this book is not a process book. It is about how to be genuinely interested in people's lives and how that helps you create feelings of comfort and trust with your customer so they buy your product. And in order for that to happen, your authenticity needs to be absolutely bulletproof.

In Barbara's case, authenticity in that moment means that once she tells you that her mom needs to find a place to move into in two days, you say, "Wow, that's fast! Then we need to move fast. We need to talk quickly and get things done quickly." That kind of message will signal to Barbara that you get it; you don't have any time to mess around here.

In this case it would be especially true that there are really only two questions we need answered. What are you most worried about? And what do you absolutely need in terms of accommodations?

You don't need to over professionalize it. You can just say, "Okay! How is your search going? What's most important to your mom? What do you need most?" Barbara's mom needs to practice walking as part of her ongoing rehab, and Barbara is worried her mom might not walk enough in a senior living community and might stay in her room all the time. So you say, "I can see why that would be a priority. Let's speak with the nurse about that at her earliest convenience. I'm sure she will have plenty of great ideas to keep your mom's rehab program intact."

YOUR AUTHENTIC BRAND PROMISE

Authenticity also needs to shine through in the way that you demonstrate your brand promise—the way you are living your brand. To do this, you need to ask yourself a few questions.

- What is your brand promise? Do you really know what your brand promise is?
- What are you doing today in the sales process that is in line with and demonstrates your brand promise?
- Would doing more things "on purpose" in line with your brand promise impact your customers in a positive way?

What your brand promise is matters, but it matters less than how well you demonstrate that promise through your interactions with every customer. Showing what life will be like when a customer moves into your community is a key differentiator and even more powerful when your brand promise is woven into your sales process, especially if there is authenticity in how you are living that brand promise through the entire sales cycle. If, for instance, you say that you offer tailored care, then your customer had better see things that are tailored when they come into your community. If your brand promise is a Vibrant Lifestyle, Quality Care, Transparency and Honesty, Independence and Dignity, or Comfort and Safety, customers need to see what that looks like and understand what that means in real life. If you say that you have a vibrant lifestyle, and that is your promise, that this is a place where seniors can have their second act, you had better have things on your programming calendar that show how seniors can actually do things that are vibrant, whether it's pursuing a degree, learning new sports, or having theme parties often.

Bringing the words of your brand promise to life will help

you stand out in the crowd of your competitors. Living your brand promise is really the essence of authenticity, because if your brand promise is strong, it cannot be replicated. Most senior living communities have a unique brand promise. Do you know yours? I held a session once on putting your brand promise to work in your sales process. When asked to share their brand promise, many shared their mission statement, but few were able to share their brand promise. Hardly anyone has the same brand promise as the community down the street. To leverage your brand promise, it is once again about the little things mattering the most. The small stuff helps them take the big step.

My partner Jessica and I worked with a salesperson recently who had done some discovery with an older couple. The wife was seventy-two and had Parkinson's, but she and her husband talked about how much they loved pickleball and how competitive they both were. Pickleball was a perfect way for her to get exercise as they found other teams who didn't mind a slower paced game. They also talked about how much they just liked to have fun. This community's brand promise was "More Active Than Ever!" Unfortunately, when she came in for the tour, the salesperson barely noted the fact that this couple had shared their love of pickleball and only briefly pointed to the pickleball court through a window while they were touring the community, saying something like, "There it is over there." What a huge missed opportunity.

On the other end of the spectrum, you can go way out of your way to demonstrate your brand promise. One community whose brand was "New Life, New Experiences" had a prospective resident who, they learned, had been the local high school's PE teacher and softball coach for twenty years. The salesperson could not get her to budge forward toward a sale. She was happy to take the pecan pie on Thanksgiving they brought her and happy to receive all the things they did to demonstrate genuine interest, but they could not get her to move forward.

Feeling frustrated, the salesperson decided to share the story with the department coordinator team. Another department coordinator asked if anyone knew how to search for old newspaper articles, because if this prospective resident coached for such a long time, there had to be some articles that they could share with her for fun.

The salesperson took that advice and found an article on the girls' high school softball team from the era in which she was the coach. In the article, pictures showed her and her team celebrating a winning season. Another department coordinator suggested that some of the residents would probably like to go to a high school softball game. The salesperson loved that idea and made a plan to ask around and find some residents who wanted to go to a high school softball game. The team decided the programming director would join the salesperson for a home visit. They brought the article they had found and asked if she would like to join several residents who were going to a high school softball game. They shared that it was no problem for them to swing their bus by her house and pick her up on the way so she could go to a softball game and meet others who love the game. That demonstrated vibrancy without a doubt and proved the brand promise of vibrancy was authentic.

PRETENDING TAKES MORE ENERGY

I've stated earlier that pretending is emotionally exhausting. If you are just pretending you care while listening to stories of people who are not in the best of situations, that is exhausting. It's so much easier when you are being your authentic self and you truly care. When you're in the moment with the customer and not always thinking about what you should ask them or tell them about next and instead just having a normal conversation, it can actually be energizing. It also allows you to leverage your time, because you're going to get your customer on board for a sale more quickly.

One marketing director I know told me a story that demonstrates this. He had a tour with a gentleman and his daughter and discovered that one of his friends, Ellen, was a resident in the same community. They hadn't seen each other in years, but the salesperson took the gentleman up to her apartment to see if she was there. Unfortunately, she was not there at the time, but this salesperson did not leave it at that. He had a strong desire to show this prospective resident something that he knew would be a true value to him, so the next day, he made a poignant video of Ellen giving a warm and welcoming review that was obviously from the heart.

Ellen ran with it, and in a beautifully authentic, sincere way told her friend what a great place this community was. She even hinted that he better hurry because the community doesn't always have available suites. It made this gentleman's day, and he moved in shortly afterward. The salesperson experienced the satisfaction of a successful sale as well as the delight of bringing joy to both Ellen and his customer's lives.

Another salesperson named Lien shared this story about a move-in to his Bethlehem, Pennsylvania, community:

Joe, a neighbor of Lien's, needed advice for a better living situation for his sister Deb, who was living in a small dark apartment with her long-time boyfriend.

Joe was concerned that Deb had been losing weight at a

rapid rate with her "miserable mister," who was a source of stress to both Joe and Deb. She had to take care of her boyfriend all the time and was doing everything for him, leaving her with no time to take care of herself.

Lien learned that Deb was looking for a hybrid senior living environment that supported freedom and independence, but one where she could still be within reach of her boyfriend. Lien consistently called Joe to check in and see how he was doing in his quest to persuade her to move. He invited Deb for a tour of his community, just to casually check it out. When she and her boyfriend visited, the chef offered them lunch, since Lien had learned Deb wasn't a fan of cooking or cleaning. Deb was unexpectedly delighted by having her and her boyfriend's meals served to her with kindness and a smile.

Deb made several more visits to the campus over the course of eight to ten months, and Joe made countless more. Lien worked with Joe to emphasize the importance of self-care to Deb. It was that significant discovery of self-worth that bonded Lien's relationship with her, and he became an adopted "family member," so to speak.

Joe and Lien were soon enjoying friendly banter on weekly texts and phone calls to coordinate Deb and her boyfriend's move. Lien highlighted the benefits of a bright, contemporary, and spacious one-bedroom deluxe apartment with a full kitchen. This was similar to the set-up of a residential home. The new space would allow her to transition more easily from a dark home. Finding the right floor plan for Deb helped her envision herself thriving in the community.

Eventually, they had moved the essential contents of their former home to create their forever home, and they took possession of the apartment. The experience of everything being set up for Deb and her boyfriend (including a fresh vase of flowers from Lien) made their move-in easier than they had ever imagined it could be.

Lien's story underscores the value of making connections with seniors and their families, which he likens to "making a super good recipe from scratch, adding dashes of intuition, advice, support, a listening ear, and unending support." The story also perfectly captures the patient, genuine caring approach that feels authentic and presents a very compelling argument for the eventual move-in. Lien thoughtfully arranged for them to see a new living space at his community that would solve many problems in Joe and Deb's life. He did this authentically, out of concern for another human being's happiness, and the result was a happy ending for everyone.

If you've learned one thing from reading this book up to this point, I hope it's that by being your authentic self, you will connect more quickly and effectively with prospective residents and their families, which will lead to closing more sales. Authenticity is truly the big red bow on the gift box of our work. It stems from a collection of strategies, approaches, and attitudes, and while it is ultimately a state of mind, it can also be learned through practice.

GET CURIOUS (IT TAKES PRACTICE)
STRENGTHENING AUTHENTICITY THROUGH
DEEPER PRODUCT KNOWLEDGE

Objective: Help salespeople enhance their authenticity with prospective residents by ensuring a deeper understanding of the community's services and offerings through collaboration with department coordinators.

Step 1: Set Up Initial Meetings with Department Heads

- Schedule individual meetings with department coordinators, such as the head of dining services, the activities director, and the head nurse. Explain that your goal is to improve how you present their department to prospective residents.
- **Example dialogue:**
  - "I'd love your input on how I'm describing your department to customers. Could you help me ensure I'm getting it right and providing an accurate picture of what your team offers?"

Step 2: Present Current Descriptions

- During each meeting, share how you currently describe their department, products, or services to customers. For example:
  - "When I speak to prospective residents, I explain that our chef can personalize meals for those with dietary restrictions. Is that accurate?"
- Ask for feedback on areas you might be missing or ways to improve the description to better align with their actual services.

Step 3: Ask Specific Questions

- Prepare a few questions for each department to ensure you fully understand their role. You might ask:
  - "What's something about your department that I may be overlooking but that's important for residents to know?"
  - "How do you handle special requests from residents, like organizing a birthday party or accommodating specific meal preferences?"

Step 4: Refine Your Descriptions

- Based on the feedback you receive, update your descriptions of each department's role, offerings, and expertise. This not only helps ensure accuracy but also gives you more confidence when discussing these services with prospective residents and their families.

Step 5: Set a Follow-Up Appointment

- After you've refined your descriptions, set a second meeting with each department head to confirm you've incorporated their feedback correctly. Ask them to listen to your revised description and provide final feedback.
- **Example dialogue:**
  - "I've updated how I explain your department to customers based on your feedback. Could I run it by you again to make sure I've captured everything accurately?"

Step 6: Build Stronger Relationships

- This process is not just about refining your knowledge, it's also about strengthening relationships with your colleagues. By reaching out to them as subject matter experts, you demonstrate that you value their expertise and are committed to presenting the community authentically.

Step 7: Document Your Findings

- After meeting with each department head, document what you've learned in your CRM or personal notes. This ensures you have accurate information to refer back to and can consistently use it in future customer interactions.

Step 8: Reflect on the Impact

- Reflect on how these conversations have improved your ability to present the community authentically. How has it changed the way you engage with prospective residents? How does it make your communication feel more genuine?

By engaging directly with the community's experts, you not only improve your product knowledge but also build credibility and authenticity with customers. You're no longer just presenting a generic sales pitch—you're offering real insights backed by the expertise of the team members who will be delivering care and services to future residents. This level of understanding sets you apart as a truly knowledgeable and authentic salesperson.

Chapter 10

Bringing It All Together to Close the Sale

"Success is in the details. It's the small stuff, the small moments, the small gestures that matter."

—HOWARD SCHULTZ

I was hesitant to add a chapter about closing, as this is not a sales process book. The concepts you've learned here can be added to any part of your sales process, and they will improve your closing ratios.

There's always a moment in the process where the salesperson feels that rapport has been built, the problems the customer presented can be solved through your solutions, and it's time to move the customer toward making a final commitment. How do we confirm that we are aligned? How do we know we've learned enough and offered solutions tailored to their needs? How do we know we've established enough value to warrant the cost?

Everything that we've talked about so far is specifically designed to help you learn as much as you can, which will allow you to comprehensively tailor a very specific solution that will be unlike any other solution a competitor can provide. For instance, helping customers feel seen and heard doesn't just improve their emotional state; when you can see and hear them, you can stay aligned with where they are in their journey.

The necessity to stay aligned with the customer is never more important than in this final step. As a salesperson working in a high-pressure environment, to increase occupancy you must stay mindful that just because you need to close a sale, the customer may not be ready. Attempting to close too soon will crush the trust you have built to get the customer this far in the decision-making process.

Consider that you have already "closed" a number of times with the customer. Every time you moved them forward up to this point, you were closing the sale, inch by inch. Moving forward in the process now is the culmination of many smaller agreements between you and the customer based on their needs and your recommendations.

You can begin to feel the alignment when customers share freely the answers to your curious questions. You know you've learned enough when the customer agrees with your recommendations. You may experience more objections as trust begins to grow, and this is a signal. You'll know you've demonstrated your value when the customer begins using future statements about specific solutions you've shared.

By letting curiosity and your listening skills take the lead during your sales process, it's likely that you will experience fewer obstacles. The tailored follow-up visit to your community and solutions offered will naturally be aligned. You listened to learn and you directly, with authenticity and transparency, built a relationship. The customer knows they matter to you. They have been seen and heard.

There is a time when, as a salesperson, you need to trust yourself as the expert. Always keep in mind, you are the expert. The customer has come to you because they have a problem and are looking to find a solution. By engaging with you, they are saying, "I want your recommendation." Through continued engagement they are saying, "You understand and care about us."

There are few things in life where a guarantee can be offered, but I will offer you this: if you slow down in your sales process, you will go fast in growing the number of customers who select your community. How can I feel so confident about this statement? If you acknowledge the enormity of the decision a customer is making and the bravery it took for them to reach out to you, if you focus on staying genuinely curious and listen with the sole intent of learning, if you consider how your words will matter, keep your promises, demonstrate your brand promise, and provide a tailored solution, you will win sales more often. You are the difference-maker when all things are equal, and you can tip the scale simply by being your authentic self.

You've got this! Now get out there and use your new skills to help make it just a bit easier for your customers to make their senior living decision.

Conclusion

"Being human is not hard because you're doing it wrong; it's hard because you're doing it right."

—GLENNON DOYLE

As we've seen throughout this journey, success in senior living sales isn't just about what you sell—it's about *how* you sell it and, more importantly, *who* you sell it to. At the heart of every interaction, we're working with families who are carrying the weight of a deeply emotional, life-altering decision. They're choosing a place that will care for someone they love—perhaps a parent who raised them, a spouse who shared their life, or another cherished individual.

We're not just selling rooms and services; we're offering solutions that will shape the quality of their loved one's life going forward. To truly help them, we must go beyond the surface level of their needs. This is where Curiosity-Driven Sales come into play.

When you approach each interaction with genuine curiosity, asking questions not just to check boxes but to truly *learn* about the individual and the family in front of you, you unlock powerful insights. You can't solve problems you don't know about, so your mission is to uncover as much as possible about what makes this person tick—what brings them joy, what frustrates them, and what will help them feel truly at home.

It's a simple truth: people need to feel seen and heard. When families are making a high-stakes, emotionally charged decision about the care of their loved ones, it's not just about choosing a facility—it's about placing their trust in you. You can honor that trust by approaching every interaction with genuine curiosity and empathy.

By taking the time to truly understand the unique details of a person's life—the little things, like their love for baking, their favorite sports team, or a proud achievement—you begin to build a real connection. Those personal stories, those details that seem small, are the very things that make individuals feel valued. In doing so, you're not just presenting a place to live; you're showing them how their parent's new home will continue to honor and embrace what makes them special.

It's not enough to be passively curious—you must listen to learn. Learn not just about their physical needs but their emotional ones as well. Every story shared, every personal detail offered, adds up to create a solution that is much more valuable.

It's through this personalized approach that trust grows. When families feel understood, they begin to believe that you are not just offering them a service but that you are genuinely committed to making sure their loved one thrives in every aspect of life—mentally, physically, and emotionally. And that's what sets you apart from the rest.

Because at the end of the day, you can't solve for what you don't know. So ask. Learn. And above all, show them that they matter. That's how you build trust, and that's how you help them choose you.

The trust built through these moments of genuine connection is what will set you apart from your competitors. You're not just a salesperson; you're a guide, a listener, a problem-solver, and, most importantly, someone who cares. When people feel that their concerns are being heard, when they know that you see them not as another sale but as a family in need of support, they begin to trust that your community will take care of their loved one in the same thoughtful, individualized way.

So, as you move forward in your career, remember that curiosity is your most powerful tool. It's the key to unlocking meaningful relationships with your customers and, ultimately, to helping them make the best decision for their loved ones.

The more you know, the more you can help. The more you can help, the more you'll close.

Acknowledgments

Writing this book has been a journey, and I could not have completed it without the support, encouragement, and contributions of many individuals.

First and foremost, my deepest gratitude goes to the sales professionals who opened their hearts and shared their personal stories with me. Your insights, challenges, and triumphs are the core of this book, and I am honored to tell your stories. Your dedication to this work inspires me every day.

I also want to express my sincere thanks to my incredible team at KJB Sales Consulting. Jessica Phaup and Brigitte Specht, your passion, expertise, and unwavering commitment have been the backbone of our mission. Your contributions to this book are invaluable, and I am so grateful for your partnership.

A special acknowledgment to Sunrise Senior Living, the organization that entrusted me with leading its sales efforts for over a decade. Your confidence in my abilities and dedication to high-quality senior care laid the groundwork for much of the insight and experience that shaped this book. I am deeply thankful for the trust, support, and opportunities that helped me grow both personally and professionally during my time there.

To my family and friends, thank you for your patience, understanding, and unending support. You gave me the time and space to complete this project, even when it meant I wasn't as present as I wanted to be.

To my mentors, colleagues, and industry peers, your guidance over the years has shaped my thinking and practice. Your wisdom is reflected throughout these pages.

Finally, to the readers—thank you for joining me on this journey of Curiosity-Driven Sales. I hope the insights and strategies within this book inspire you to create meaningful connections and achieve greater success.

Thank you all, from the bottom of my heart.

Stay Curious,
Kelly Singleton Myers

www.ingramcontent.com/pod-product-compliance
Lightning Source LLC
Chambersburg PA
CBHW071555210326
41597CB00019B/3254